Suicide

Suicide

Other Books in the Current Controversies Series:

Suicide

Leslie A. Miller, *Book Editor*
Paul A. Rose, *Book Editor*

David Bender, *Publisher*
Bruno Leone, *Executive Editor*

Bonnie Szumski, *Editorial Director*
David M. Haugen, *Managing Editor*

CURRENT CONTROVERSIES

Cover photo: © Tony Stone Images/Jon Bradley

Library of Congress Cataloging-in-Publication Data

Suicide / Leslie A. Miller, Paul A. Rose, book editors.
    p. cm. — (Current controversies)
    Includes bibliographical references and index.
    ISBN 0-7377-0317-2 (pbk. : alk. paper). — ISBN 0-7377-0318-0
(lib. : alk. paper)
    1. Suicide. I. Miller, Leslie A. II. Rose, Paul A. III. Series.
HV6545 .S818   2000
362.28—dc21
                                                          99-053091
                                                              CIP

©2000 by Greenhaven Press, Inc., PO Box 289009, San Diego, CA 92198-9009
Printed in the U.S.A.

Every effort has been made to trace the owners of copyrighted material.

Contents

Chapter 1: Is Suicide an Individual Right?

Yes: Suicide Is an Individual Right

No: Suicide Is Not an Individual Right

✳ Chapter 2: What Are the Causes of Suicide?

Chapter 3: Should Physicians Help Terminally Ill Patients Commit Suicide?

Yes: The Terminally Ill Have a Right to Physician-Assisted Suicide

No: Physicians Should Not Help Terminally Ill Patients Commit Suicide

Chapter 4: How Can Suicide Be Prevented?

Foreword

By definition, controversies are "discussions of questions in which opposing opinions clash" (Webster's Twentieth Century Dictionary Unabridged). Few would deny that controversies are a pervasive part of the human condition and exist on virtually every level of human enterprise. Controversies transpire between individuals and among groups, within nations and between nations. Controversies supply the grist necessary for progress by providing challenges and challengers to the status quo. They also create atmospheres where strife and warfare can flourish. A world without controversies would be a peaceful world; but it also would be, by and large, static and prosaic.

The Series' Purpose

The purpose of the Current Controversies series is to explore many of the social, political, and economic controversies dominating the national and international scenes today. Titles selected for inclusion in the series are highly focused and specific. For example, from the larger category of criminal justice, Current Controversies deals with specific topics such as police brutality, gun control, white collar crime, and others. The debates in Current Controversies also are presented in a useful, timeless fashion. Articles and book excerpts included in each title are selected if they contribute valuable, long-range ideas to the overall debate. And wherever possible, current information is enhanced with historical documents and other relevant materials. Thus, while individual titles are current in focus, every effort is made to ensure that they will not become quickly outdated. Books in the Current Controversies series will remain important resources for librarians, teachers, and students for many years.

In addition to keeping the titles focused and specific, great care is taken in the editorial format of each book in the series. Book introductions and chapter prefaces are offered to provide background material for readers. Chapters are organized around several key questions that are answered with diverse opinions representing all points on the political spectrum. Materials in each chapter include opinions in which authors clearly disagree as well as alternative opinions in which authors may agree on a broader issue but disagree on the possible solutions. In this way, the content of each volume in Current Controversies mirrors the mosaic of opinions encountered in society. Readers will quickly realize that there are many viable answers to these complex issues. By questioning each author's conclusions, students and casual readers can begin to develop the critical thinking skills so important to evaluating opinionated material.

Current Controversies is also ideal for controlled research. Each anthology in the series is composed of primary sources taken from a wide gamut of informational categories including periodicals, newspapers, books, United States and foreign government documents, and the publications of private and public organizations. Readers will find factual support for reports, debates, and research papers covering all areas of important issues. In addition, an annotated table of contents, an index, a book and periodical bibliography, and a list of organizations to contact are included in each book to expedite further research.

Perhaps more than ever before in history, people are confronted with diverse and contradictory information. During the Persian Gulf War, for example, the public was not only treated to minute-to-minute coverage of the war, it was also inundated with critiques of the coverage and countless analyses of the factors motivating U.S. involvement. Being able to sort through the plethora of opinions accompanying today's major issues, and to draw one's own conclusions, can be a complicated and frustrating struggle. It is the editors' hope that Current Controversies will help readers with this struggle.

Greenhaven Press anthologies primarily consist of previously published material taken from a variety of sources, including periodicals, books, scholarly journals, newspapers, government documents, and position papers from private and public organizations. These original sources are often edited for length and to ensure their accessibility for a young adult audience. The anthology editors also change the original titles of these works in order to clearly present the main thesis of each viewpoint and to explicitly indicate the opinion presented in the viewpoint. These alterations are made in consideration of both the reading and comprehension levels of a young adult audience. Every effort is made to ensure that Greenhaven Press accurately reflects the original intent of the authors included in this anthology.

Introduction

Suicide is a serious problem that is becoming a national crisis. In 1997, the most recent year for which statistics are available, 30,535 Americans committed suicide. This is equivalent to one person every 17.2 minutes, making suicide the eighth leading cause of death in the United States. Suicide has recently become the second leading cause of death among people under twenty-five.

Researchers have long struggled to understand why people kill themselves. Most agree that people who commit suicide usually do so when they are already in a stressful situation—often referred to as a "risk factor"—and something happens to trigger the act.

Risk factors for suicide include depression, drug and alcohol dependency, life inexperience, an inability to solve problems, a history of sexual abuse, and many others. Of these risk factors, depression is generally considered the most serious. Stephen L. Bernhardt, an expert on suicide, explains how depression distorts reality and creates feelings of hopelessness:

> Depression causes us to narrow our view of the world around us to such an extent that reality becomes distorted. The negative in our lives is constantly reinforced and the positive around us is discounted as being irrelevant, or even nonexistent. Options to help solve our problems are rejected as having no merit, until it seems as if there is no possible solution. An unrelenting and oppressive sadness comes over us which causes a very real pain, as if the pain of the sudden loss of a parent stays with us for weeks, months, and even years. It is as if we are trapped in a dark cave or possibly a tunnel that runs only from our constant pain to somewhere near hell, with no exit to heaven and no exit to joy. We begin to think that there is no relief and that this pain will never end. Tomorrow will be the same, or worse. Death may be the only solution!

Some experts contend that depression and the suicidal feelings that can accompany it are exacerbated by substance abuse. Although the National Clearinghouse for Alcohol and Drug Information denies a direct cause-and-effect relationship between suicide and the use of alcohol and other drugs, it holds that

> such use often is a contributing factor. . . . Drinking, use of other drugs, or both may reduce inhibitions and impair the judgment of someone contemplating suicide, making the act more likely. And use of [alcohol or drugs] also

may aggravate other risk factors for suicide such as depression or other mental illness. . . . Between 20 and 35 percent of suicide victims had a history of alcohol abuse or were drinking shortly before their suicides.

Just as depression and substance abuse change the way a person views life's problems and accomplishments, so does adolescence. The teenage years and early twenties are a difficult period for many, and the high suicide rate for this age group is a reflection of this. Adolescents are at risk of suicide because their youth and inexperience may blind them to possible solutions to their problems. George Howe Colt in his book *The Enigma of Suicide* maintains that young people kill themselves for any number of reasons:

> the unraveling of America's moral fiber, the breakdown of the nuclear family, school pressure, peer pressure, parental pressure, parental lassitude, child abuse, drugs, alcohol, low blood sugar, TV, MTV, popular music (rock, punk, or Heavy Metal, depending on the decade), promiscuity, lagging church attendance, increased violence, racism, . . . the threat of nuclear war, the media, rootlessness, increased affluence, unemployment, capitalism, excessive freedom, boredom, narcissism, . . . disillusionment with government, lack of heroes, movies about suicide, too much discussion of suicide, too little discussion of suicide.

Some researchers, however, argue that teens kill themselves for different reasons than those suggested by Colt. Mike A. Males, in his book *The Scapegoat Generation: America's War on Adolescents*, argues that juvenile suicide often results from injuries caused by parents and others. He points to a list of causes that are fundamentally different from those presented by Colt:

> The reasons for their suicidal feelings often are not comfortable for adults to contemplate. One of the biggest is a history of sexual abuse. . . . [Other] key factors in suicide incidence are maleness, homosexuality, economic stress, childhood neglect and violence, and individual biochemistry. Most of these factors cannot be changed by changes in social environments and attitudes.

Because depression and the travails of adolescence can keep individuals from seeing alternatives to suicide, these risk factors make people more likely to commit suicide when a trigger event occurs. Suicidologist Lollie McLain clarifies the relationship between stressful situations and trigger events: "Imagine a big refrigerator sitting on a porch. How easy is it to move? Not very. But if it's on one edge teetering . . . now how easy is it to tip it either way?"

The most common events that may trigger someone to commit suicide are the death of a friend or family member, the breakup of a romantic relationship, difficulties in school or at work, conflicts with others, physical impairment, and other people's suicides. CRUMBS, an online youth magazine, points out that "usually youth suicide is not caused by any one factor, but by an accumulation of the various factors through childhood and adolescence. As such, there are no easy answers and cure alls."

Although an awareness of risk factors and trigger events can help suicide prevention professionals understand and prevent suicide, the causes of suicide are never entirely clear-cut. No one knows exactly why some people cope successfully with certain risk factors and trigger events, while others turn to suicide. The authors represented in this book, *Suicide: Current Controversies,* discuss the question of why people commit suicide, along with other controversial aspects of this complex and tragic issue.

Chapter 1

Is Suicide an Individual Right?

Chapter Preface

Libertarians and others who want to keep government out of people's lives argue that everyone has the right to commit suicide—at any time and for any reason—because people own their own bodies. As Libertarian Party chairman Steve Dasbach contends, "Like the right to life, [the right to die] is a basic human right that predates the Constitution and is protected by it. It can be neither granted nor taken away."

At the opposite extreme, the Roman Catholic Church, one of the most influential opponents of suicide, holds that people's bodies belong to God and therefore no one ever has the right to commit suicide. In his 1995 encyclical letter *Evangelium Vitae*, Pope John Paul II writes:

> Suicide is always as morally objectionable as murder. The Church's tradition has always rejected it as a gravely evil choice. Even though a certain psychological, cultural and social conditioning may induce a person to carry out an action which so radically contradicts the innate inclination to life, thus lessening or removing subjective responsibility, suicide . . . is a gravely immoral act. . . . Suicide represents a rejection of God's absolute sovereignty over life and death.

This conflicting ideology about whether people's lives belong to God or to themselves is the cornerstone of the ethical debate about suicide. Viewpoints in this chapter consider these and other arguments related to the individual's right to commit suicide.

People Have the Right to Commit Suicide

by Walter Williams

About the author: *Walter Williams is a syndicated columnist.*

Making our value premises explicit and clear can help untangle contentious public policy issues or at least let us know where people stand. Let's state my personal value premise. I cherish private property rights. "OK," you say, "but what are private property rights?"

The Owner Is Responsible

Private property rights refer to an owner's right to acquire, keep, use and dispose of property in ways that do not violate the property rights of others. If that's a shared value, there's little debate on a whole class of public policy issues. Let's see.

I am the property of Walter Williams. Among other things, that means I have the right to take chances with my own life but not that of others.

Mandating that I wear a seat belt violates my rights, whereas drunk-driving laws and vehicle-safety inspection laws don't. Choosing not to wear a seat belt raises my risk of death. That's my right. Driving drunk or driving an unsafe car raises the risk of harming others. That's not my right.

"Williams," you say, "we gotcha this time. If you don't wear a seat belt and wind up a vegetable, you burden society, which has to take care of you." That's not a problem of private property rights; it's a problem of socialism (weakened private property rights). People's money belongs to them. They shouldn't be forced to take care of me.

This term [1996], the U.S. Supreme Court is taking up the "right to die" issue. Private property rights can illuminate. Pretend it's the United States vs. Williams.

First, the Court should determine just who owns Williams. The evidence will show that while some of my ancestors were owned, my mother and father were not. Since Williams has attained 21 years of age, it would seem that he owns himself. That finding of self-ownership would make the Court's task easy.

Reprinted from "Private Rights Versus Public Rights," by Walter Williams, *Headway,* December 1996. Reprinted with permission from Creator's Syndicate.

Their 9–0 decision would read: Though the thought of Williams ending his precious life is distasteful and while the loss of his insightful weekly columns will be a great loss to society, nonetheless, we find he owns himself and has the right to dispose of his life in any manner consistent with the safety of others.

There'd be a different decision if I didn't own myself. The first complexity would be to find out just who owns Williams. But let's fudge that complexity by saying that Congress owns him.

If Congress Owned Williams

That being the case, I wouldn't have the right to take chances with my life. Congress would have every right to force me to use a seat belt. Moreover, it would have the right to force me to stop smoking, exercise, get plenty of rest and restrict my dietary intake of salt, cholesterol and alcohol. In *United States vs. Williams,* the court would rightfully decree that I had no right to dispose of Williams. After all, that would be destroying government property.

I disagree with the ways some people "unwisely" use their property. Many drink and smoke too much, wear gaudy attire, become couch potatoes and don't buckle up when they drive. But the true test of one's commitment to liberty and private property rights doesn't come when we permit people to be free to do those voluntary things with which we agree. The true test comes when we permit people to be free to do those voluntary things with which we disagree.

> *"I am the property of Walter Williams."*

Undoubtedly, my position is offensive to many, and mankind's history is on their side. Private property rights and self-determination have always received a hostile reception. People have always had what they consider to be good reasons for restricting the liberties of others.

Suicide Is Sometimes Permissible

by Victor Cosculluela

About the author: *Victor Cosculluela is the author of* The Ethics of Suicide.

Authors from various disciplines have brought forth reasons for preventing all, or at least virtually all, suicide. We will consider these arguments in an attempt to determine whether or not, and in what circumstances, others should prevent a suicide from realizing his intentions. We shall reach a moderate conclusion: some suicide may legitimately be prevented, but not all. Arguments for the view that all suicide should be prevented are unacceptable. . . .

Preventing Suicide

I will assume that totally uncoercive suicide prevention measures need no justification. For example, merely presenting the would-be suicide with one's antisuicide position requires no justification. Suggesting a psychotherapist for the person who seeks relief from his suicidal impulses also requires no justification. For the remainder of this viewpoint I will have in mind coercive preventive measures (e.g., involuntary hospitalization, medication, etc.). . . .

Psychological Arguments

Mental Illness: By far the most important psychological argument with respect to suicide prevention is the claim that suicide prevention is justified since suicide is always or at least virtually always a manifestation of some form of mental illness. We are told by Erwin Ringel that the suicidal option is almost always chosen under "pathological circumstances or under the influence of diseased feelings." Further, George Murphy asserts that so-called "rational" suicide is a rarity since most persons who commit suicide are "suffering from clinically recognizable psychiatric illnesses often carrying an excellent prognosis." From this some are led to infer that the therapist must not only make clear to the patient that, in the words of Alan Stone, he "believes such behavior arises from the patient's illness"; he must "do everything he can to prevent it, enlisting

Excerpted from *The Ethics of Suicide,* by Victor Cosculluela (Camden, CT: Garland Publishing, 1995). Reprinted with permission from the publisher and the author. Footnotes in the original have been omitted.

the rest of the staff in this effort." Further, the claim is made that suicidal intent "must not be part of therapeutic confidentiality in a hospital setting."

However, there is a great deal of disagreement on the relation between suicide and mental illness. First, even some of those who accept the claim that perhaps most of those who attempt suicide are, as John Moskop and Tristram Engelhardt write, "limited in their ability to think and act rationally by some mental illness" admit that "it would be extremely difficult" to justify the claim that all suicide attempts are products of mental illness. Further, psychiatrist Thomas Szasz claims that the view that suicide is a manifestation of mental illness is "both erroneous and evil": erroneous since "it treats an act as if it were a happening"; and evil because it "serves to legitimize psychiatric force and fraud by justifying it as medical care and treatment." Finally, some psychiatrists take a moderate view, regarding many suicides as mentally ill, while allowing that many make realistic estimations of their options. It is therefore not surprising that after examining the psychiatric material pertaining to suicide, Margaret Battin reaches the following conclusion: "There is clearly no consensus on the frequency of mental illness in suicide or suicide attempts"; in fact, estimates of the percentage of mentally ill among suicides have ranged from as low as 20% to as high as 100%. However, one point on which there is widespread agreement is that relatively few suicides are psychotic. (It would be ironic if most suicides were psychotic since, on some estimates, the suicide rate for psychiatrists is almost seven times that of the general population.)

No Justification

Even if we accept the claim that the desire to commit suicide is a manifestation of some form of mental illness, that *in itself* would not justify preventive measures. The desire to produce a comprehensive metaphysical system might be (and no doubt has been) a manifestation of mental illness, but that in itself would not justify others in preventing its realization. Even the desire to recover from one's mental illness might be a by-product of the illness, but surely no one would suggest that this justifies perpetuating the patient's illness. So even if one could show that all suicidal desires are products of mental illness (which is clearly not the case), that alone would not justify preventive measures.

> *"Some suicide may legitimately be prevented, but not all. Arguments for the view that all suicide should be prevented are unacceptable."*

Although these examples show that the fact that a desire arises from mental illness is not *in itself* sufficient to justify the coercive prevention of its realization, one might claim that the self-harming aspect of suicide, when combined with the presence of mental illness, justifies the coercive prevention of suicide. However, even this claim is false, for we do not always consider it appropriate to prevent those with mental illnesses from realizing their desires, even when those desires are related to their illnesses and their fulfillment would cause the agent harm. For example, even if we discovered that a person's religious practices (e.g., fasting) were due in part to some minor neurosis, we would not (other-regarding factors aside) consider it appropriate to prevent the person from engaging in these practices, even if such practices were harmful to the agent. . . .

The Cry for Help

A second psychological thesis that is used to justify coercive suicide prevention measures asserts that potential suicides wish to be saved; suicidal behavior is a "cry for help." Suicidologist Edwin Shneidman is the main proponent of this view: "Individuals who are intent on killing themselves still wish very much to be rescued or to have their deaths prevented." Consequently, suicide prevention consists essentially in recognizing that the potential suicide is ambivalent between his wishes to live and his wishes to die, then "throwing one's efforts on the side of life."

> *"Relatively few suicides are psychotic."*

This attempt to justify coercive suicide prevention measures is problematic. In support of this view, one might appeal to the fact that a high percentage of would-be suicides appreciate being saved. However, this would only provide a limited defense since some survivors express bitterness over their "rescue." Further, it is doubtful that those who attempt to commit suicide in ways that make it easy for others to save them fall into the same class as those who attempt suicide in ways which make it nearly impossible for others to save them. The claim that someone who committed suicide by firing a shotgun into his mouth was communicating a desperate "cry for help" seems quite implausible; it is unlikely that those who want to be rescued would make it virtually impossible for others to rescue them.

However, there is an even more serious problem with the cry for help justification of coercive suicide prevention measures. Shneidman's view is that potential suicides have serious doubts about suicide even though they also have pro-attitudes toward suicide. However, this in itself does not justify suicide prevention. Whenever one makes a difficult choice, it is likely that one will still have doubts, but this in itself does not show that others are justified in preventing us from carrying out our decisions. When somebody makes a career choice, he may have serious doubts about the wisdom of his choice, but such doubts do not allow others to prevent him from carrying out his choice. . . .

The Transitoriness of the Suicidal Desire

A third psychological thesis, which is repeated quite frequently in the literature, claims that the wish to die by suicide is usually fleeting: "The desire to terminate one's life is usually transient. The 'right' to suicide is a 'right' desired only temporarily," Murphy writes. From this a momentous conclusion is immediately reached: "Every physician should feel the obligation to support the desire for life."

Here again it would be a mistake to use an invalid argument of the following form: since most potential suicides have a certain characteristic, this in itself justifies treating all potential suicides as if they had that characteristic. Even if the desire for suicide is transient in most cases, that in itself will not justify the claim that all suicide should be prevented. One can easily imagine cases in which individuals think long and hard on the suicidal option before embracing it.

> *"Even if the desire for suicide is transient in most cases, that in itself will not justify the claim that all suicide should be prevented."*

Further, why should the simple fact that a desire is transient justify others in preventing its realization? The desire to do something very good for others might be fleeting, but that in itself does not show that others are justified in preventing its realization. Clearly, the lifespan of a desire does not *in itself* determine whether or not one should prevent its realization, otherwise one would have to say that a transitory desire to do good for others must be frustrated.

The appeal to the claim that *most* suicide results from mental illness, the appeal to the alleged ambivalence of *most* suicides, and the appeal to the alleged transitoriness of *most* suicidal impulses all fail to justify the claim that *all* suicide should be prevented. Further, since the mere fact that a desire springs from mental illness, the mere fact that one is ambivalent about it, and the mere fact it is fleeting are each insufficient to show that the desire's realization should be prevented, it turns out that appealing to mental illness, ambivalence, or to the fleeting nature of suicidal impulses will not *in itself* justify suicide prevention *in any case whatsoever*. Further, even if one made an appeal to all three claims (i.e., the mental illness claim, the ambivalence claim, and the transitoriness claim), it seems that that in itself would not justify any preventive measures. Why, then, have so many authors repeatedly appealed to these alleged facts in an attempt to justify coercive suicide prevention measures?

Beliefs Are Relevant

With respect to the mental illness claim, the reason may be that mental illness is related to something else which is relevant to the question of suicide prevention: the potential suicide's factual (non-moral) beliefs. Whether or not someone has correct factual beliefs is relevant to the issue of paternalistic interference. If, for example, laymen want to take certain drugs in the belief that they will be cured of their ailments, when in fact they would be seriously harmed, laws which attempt to prevent them from obtaining the drugs without prescriptions may be justified. Mental illness enters the picture when we realize the impact it can have on one's factual beliefs; depending on the severity of the illness, one might come to hold ludicrous factual beliefs. For example, one might come to believe the following: "Unless I kill myself, I'll become a werewolf." In cases where mental illness creates factual ignorance which gives rise to suicidal intentions, suicide prevention may be justified. Even in such a case, it would be inaccurate to say that the presence of mental illness justifies preventive measures; the factual errors justify preventive measures; the mental illness simply happens in this case to be responsible for the factual ignorance which is partially responsible for the desire to commit suicide.

Mental illness is also relevant when it prevents someone from acting on his deepest desires, even though it may not involve factual ignorance. One might, for example, be the victim of irrational fears or compulsions which push one toward self-destruction, even though one may also have a rationally formed desire to live. In such cases, preventive measures seem justified. (It should be noted, however, that . . . it is unclear that self-destruction due to compulsions counts as suicide.)

Ambivalence and Transience

As for the appeals to ambivalence (the cry for help model) and the alleged transitoriness of suicidal desires, these claims seem relevant to factual beliefs about one's deepest desires; if one is ambivalent, one may say, "I don't know what I want," and transitory desires often create confusion about what one "really" desires. Paternalistic prevention measures may be justified by the potential suicide's ignorance about his own deepest desires. However, it would be incorrect to say that the ambivalence alone, or the transitoriness alone, justifies preventive measures; rather, factual ignorance which would otherwise be likely to cause self-harm justifies paternalistic preventive measures. Ambivalence and transitoriness are relevant only as possible sources of ignorance.

One might claim that transitoriness is itself directly relevant to the issue of whether preventive measures would be justified in cases of potential suicide. After all, one may *really* want *now* to kill oneself. However, if this desire would only last for, say, a minute, it may seem that that in itself is relevant to the issue of suicide prevention.

It seems to me that if the transitory desire for suicide accompanied (perhaps by causing) the mistaken belief that the desire is enduring, that would

> *"It would be inaccurate to say that the presence of mental illness justifies preventive measures."*

indeed be relevant, but only because that would be an instance of factual error. (Presumably, most people would not act on their suicidal impulses if they were aware of the transitoriness of these impulses.) However, one might press the point by proposing a highly unusual case in which a potential suicide *really* wants to kill himself yet is fully aware that this desire is fleeting. If our potential suicide realizes that his suicidal desire is fleeting and if he is in control of himself, then, unless other-regarding factors are at stake, it seems to me that we are not entitled to prevent his suicide. (I am assuming here that would-be preventers know that the potential suicide has the knowledge and self-control in question.) . . . The potential suicide knows that he genuinely wants to kill himself, he knows that his desire is fleeting, and yet he still wants to fulfill the desire. Why should the mere fact that the desire is transient matter in this case when it does not matter in other cases (e.g., cases in which one has transient desires to do tremendous good for society)?

It might be said that in cases of suicidal desire, the transient desire would be terminal if fulfilled. But if death is precisely what the person wants, and if he knows that this desire is fleeting, I fail to see how the *mere* fact of transitoriness counts. Transitoriness is related to factual ignorance (e.g., it may mask one's deeper desires and it might create the illusion that the transitory desire for suicide is actually an enduring desire), but it is only because of this relation that it is relevant to the suicide prevention issue. . . .

Other-Regarding Considerations

So far we have focused only on the would-be suicide. One might, however, try to defend suicide prevention measures on the ground that suicide involves deep suffering for others (e.g., the suicide's family and friends). Naturally, one will have to balance this suffering against the negative features of preventive measures; we are not entitled to prevent people from acting in certain ways on the ground that others would be slightly annoyed otherwise. Further, this justification of suicide prevention will not apply to those would-be suicides who do not have important relations to others.

None of the arguments considered justifies preventive measures in all cases of potential suicide. The psychological arguments from mental illness, transitoriness, and ambivalence turned out to be only indirectly relevant; such features alone never justify preventive measures, but they are relevant to the would-be suicide's factual beliefs and self-control. In that sense, mental illness, ambivalence, and the presence of transitory suicidal impulses are indirectly relevant to the issue of suicide prevention. . . . Finally, the argument which tries to justify suicide prevention measures by appealing to other-regarding considerations will justify some instances of prevention, but not all.

The Bible Does Not Condemn Suicide

by Gene Kasmar

About the author: *Gene Kasmar is the author of the book* All the Obscenities in the Bible.

One can hardly pick up a newspaper today without encountering the latest reports about Dr. Kevorkian's assisted suicide antics. One can also be sure to detect a "media" bias and abhorrence of various facets of suicide. Although why this should be so in our modern and so-called Judeo-Christian culture should be the larger question.

After all, other than the general biblical admonition that "Thou shalt not kill," euthanasia and "suicide" are nowhere condemned, proscribed, nor censured in that holy book. Because many consider the Bible to be the source of all morality and law, the oversight is certainly significant. Instead, the Bible treats the many suicides found within as honorable acts, and always preferable to the alternatives.

For starters, take the euthanasia case of Moses' brother Aaron. At the age of 123 (Biblical) years he was taken atop Mt. Hor by his brother and his son, stripped of his clothing, and left to die while Moses and Eleazar awaited his end (Numbers 20:22–29). Mt. Hor is somewhere in the Edomite chain of mile-high peaks, a very severe environment with often snow capped peaks. Shortly thereafter it was Moses' turn atop Mt. Nebo. Moses went to his death even though his ". . . eye was not dim, nor his natural force abated." (Deuteronomy 34:1–7). In other words, he was still sexually active.

King Saul's Suicide

We next read that King Saul commits suicide (As does his armor-bearer too!), in ". . . Saul tells his armor-bearer to draw your sword, and thrust me through with it lest the uncircumcised come and thrust me through . . . but his armor-bearer would not. Therefore Saul took his own sword and fell upon it. And

Reprinted from "Suicide, an Ethical and Moral Alternative," by Gene Kasmar, *The Human Quest,* May/June 1997. Reprinted with permission.

when his armor-bearer saw that Saul was dead, he did likewise, and died with him. So Saul died." (I Samuel 31:4–6, and I Chronicles 10:4–6).

Unfortunately, that account contradicts a friendly Amalekite later telling David that ". . . Saul said to me, stand beside me and slay me; for anguish has seized me and yet my life still lingers. So I stood beside him and slew him, because I was sure that he could not live after he had fallen." (2 Samuel 1:6–10).

A second assisted suicide occurs when King Abimelech had been severely wounded because a woman dropped a stone upon his head. He then said to his armor-bearer ". . . draw your sword and kill me, lest men say 'A woman killed him'. . . and he thrust him through and he died." (Judges 9:54). Now, although Abimelech had already annoyed God by killing his 70 brothers (!), no censure revolves around the method by which he chose to die.

Other willful suicides in the Bible include Samson (Judges 16:29–30), Ahithophel (by hanging, 2 Samuel 17:23), King Zimri (by immolation, I Kings 16: 17–18), and of course Judas (by hanging, Matthew 27:5). Judas also undergoes a second (and apparently accidental) death in the book of Acts 1:16–17, when ". . . falling headlong, he burst open in the middle and all his bowels gushed out." None of these suicides resulted in any Biblical reproach or censure based upon the mode of death selected.

In the Apocrypha are found several more suicides including the heroic Eleazar who noticed that one of the enemy elephants ". . . was equipped with royal armor and taller than the others . . . so he gave his life to save his people and to win for himself an everlasting name . . . he got under and stabbed the elephant from beneath . . . it fell upon him and he died." (I Maccabees 6:43–46). This is one of the earliest known incidents of "suicide by elephant."

Jesus Speaks of Suicide

In the Bible, we also have Jesus (the sacrificial lamb!) threatening suicide on several occasions, as in "Then said the Jews, will he kill himself?, because he saith, whither I go, ye cannot come." (John 8:22), and later ". . . I lay down my life for the sheep . . . no one takes my life from me, but I lay it down of my own accord." (John 10:15–18). We have Jesus also saying ". . . the son of man came . . . to serve, and to give his life as a ransom . . ." (Mark 10:45), and "Greater love has no man . . . to lay down his life for his friends." (John 15:13).

> *"Other than the general biblical admonition that 'Thou shalt not kill,' euthanasia and 'suicide' are nowhere condemned, proscribed, nor censured in that holy book."*

Although some might see some ambiguity in these passages, the authoritative church father, St. Augustine, wrote that Jesus' spirit departed because he willed it to happen and he willed when and how it would happen.

There is much more of the same, but nowhere is found any opprobrium, condemnation, or prohibition associated with suicide and euthanasia throughout the whole Bible.

In the Judeo-Christian tradition, suicide-by-martyrdom is considered among the most noble acts a believer can perform. Consider the record itself: the 960 suicides at Masada in 73 A.D., the mass suicide of about 150 Jews at York, England in 1190 to avoid forced conversion, the holy virgins venerated as saints who killed themselves to defend their virtue, the Christian martyrs who embraced death willingly, the 950 deaths at Jonestown in 1978, the 84 Branch Davidian deaths at Waco, Texas, the 32 Solar Temple suicides in Europe and Canada, and so on.

> *"Willful suicides in the Bible include Samson, . . . Ahithophel, . . . King Zimri, . . . and of course Judas."*

In conclusion then, any censure of self-imposed or assisted suicide stems only from extra-biblical theology, dogma, and opinions imposed by sectarian fiat, and not from the words and content of the Bible itself. Self-willed death remains a morally acceptable and ethical option in the context of the divinely revealed and inspired Judeo-Christian holy book, the Bible. It is long past time that theologians honestly shared that information with their followers.

Suicide Can Be a Rational Choice

by Margaret Pabst Battin

About the author: *Margaret Pabst Battin, a professor of philosophy at the University of Utah, is the author of the book* Ethical Issues in Suicide, *from which this viewpoint is extracted.*

Although traditional moral arguments still inform many of the precritical assumptions we make about suicide, they have fallen into disuse. In the twentieth century we have tended to treat suicide as the product of mental illness, as a desperate and dangerous cry for help used by someone who does not really want to die, or, more recently, as the result of altered neurobiological states. These views suggest that the traditional moral arguments no longer have relevance either for persons contemplating suicide or for bystanders who would intervene. But these views sidestep a crucial issue: Can suicide ever be a *rational* act? If so, we may need to reconsider our moral assessment of suicide. That an act is rational does not mean, of course, that it is also morally good, but to find potentially rational an act we had thought could only be crazy may invite reinspection of our views.

Can suicide ever be rational? Perhaps none of our acts are ever *wholly* rational, in that they are never wholly free from emotion, training, circumstantial coercion, or other arational components, yet we readily distinguish between things that we choose rationally to do, or that it is rational for us to do, and alternative acts that could be done in the same circumstance but are not rational acts. The question, then, is this: Can suicide be as rational as our other rational acts? Are there special conditions for rationality when the issue is ending life? . . .

We shall attempt to construct a set of criteria for rationality. . . .

These criteria fall into two broad groups. The first three are included in the group of what might be called *nonimpairment* criteria: ability to reason, realistic world view, and adequacy of information. The final two—avoidance of harm and accordance with fundamental interests—are included in the group of what might be called the _satisfaction of interests_ criteria: A rational decision is seen as one that serves the agent's own interests, both in avoiding harm and achieving his or her goals. We typically speak of a decision as rational or rationally made if it is made in an unimpaired way; we also speak of a decision as rational or as the rational thing for someone to do if it satisfies his or her interests in avoiding harm and achieving his or her goals. The question of rational suicide, then, may be restated as a compound issue: Can suicide be chosen in a rational way, and can it be a rational thing for a particular person to do? . . .

The Ability to Reason

Traditionally, a rational person has been defined as one who has the use of reason, or the ability to reason; a rational decision is one in the reaching of which reason is employed. But to say that a person is able to reason implies at least two distinct things: (1) that in moving from the premises from which he or she begins to the conclusion reached, he or she maintains good logical form— that is, the person does not make mistakes in logic—and (2) that the person can see the consequences of the positions he or she adopts or of the actions he or she plans to take.

Suicidologists Shneidman and Farberow have examined a large number of suicide notes collected from the Los Angeles County Coroner's Office, and on this basis attempt to re-create what they call _suicidal thinking_. Suicidal thinking, they claim, involves both syntactic and semantic fallacies, the most characteristic of which is a confusion between "oneself as experienced by oneself," and "oneself as experienced by others." For instance, in the quite typical bit of reasoning "People who kill themselves get attention; I will kill myself; therefore I will get attention," the prospective suicide uses the pronoun 'I' to refer to himself _as experienced by himself_ in the second premise, but in the conclusion he uses it to refer to himself _as he will be experienced by others_ after he is dead. What this equivocation disguises is the fact that the 'I' who is now doing the experiencing and is now eager for attention is not the same 'I' as the one who will get attention: after death, the 'I' who now craves attention will not be present to experience it.

This error in reasoning is very closely related to the second condition for 'being able to reason': a person who has the use of reason is one who can see, at least to some degree, not only the logical but also the causal consequences of his or her beliefs, statements, and actions. Thus, a person who commits rational suicide must be able to foresee the probable consequences of his or her act of suicide, both for others and for himself or herself. It may, of course, be very difficult to foresee with full accuracy the impact of one's suicide on others, but there is one

> *"Can suicide be chosen in a rational way, and can it be a rational thing for a particular person to do?"*

consequence of suicide that can be foreseen with certainty: The individual who commits suicide will be dead.

But this is precisely what a great many suicides do not accurately foresee; they tend to assume that even after death, they will continue to have experiences, to interact with other persons, and to play some continuing causal role in the world. This is characteristic of psychotic suicides. Some researchers also suggest that almost all child suicides are "irrational" in this way. Influenced perhaps by television and cartoon figures who die but revive unharmed, children are not able to think of themselves as dead, but instead think of the death that follows suicide as a kind of sleep from which they will reawaken intact. . . .

Dyadic Suicide

Most common among the errors in reasoning committed by those who kill themselves or attempt to do so, however, may be the kind of assumption underlying much of so-called dyadic suicide. In these suicides the intention of the individual is to injure, manipulate, insult, or impress the important other person in his or her life. "I'll get even with you," is an expression typical of the dyadic suicide; so is "I'll make you love me after all," or "I'll make you finally see how much you really need me." But this kind of assumption, some suicidologists claim, is fundamentally irrational in suicide contexts, since if the gesture is effective there will be no "I" to appreciate that fact.

Most suicide attempts, and some completed suicides, are of this dyadic form, and are thus subject to the kind of fallacy in reasoning that such motivation invites. But this does not establish that all cases of this type of suicide are irrational. A person may in fact succeed in "getting even" with another even though he or she is no longer available to appreciate that fact: For instance, an intolerant parent may get even with a wayward child by striking the child from his or her will, even though the will does not go into effect until after the parent has died. Similarly we can imagine cases in which a person intends to get even with someone else by suicide, even though he or she knows that it will be impossible to savor this success and that his or her own sacrifice will be great. Although such cases may be infrequent, they can in principle occur.

> *"After death, the 'I' who now craves attention will not be present to experience it."*

There are, in addition, two important classes of suicides that are not necessarily irrational. First, for those individuals whose religious or metaphysical beliefs include the possibility of a sentient afterlife, it is not irrational (though it might be false) to assume that one will have continuing experiences or relationships after suicide. And, second, some individuals place little or no value on themselves as subjects of experiences or participants in relationships, but place great importance on the ways in which they are viewed by others. Typically, reputation and honor are paramount to these individuals; continuing experience is not. These individuals too rarely confuse the notion that they will be viewed in a certain way after death with the erroneous notion that they will be able to observe or experience this view; such suicides are not irrational in this respect. . . .

A Realistic World View

We may assume that a rational decision is based upon a realistic view of the world; this criterion is closely related to that of ability to reason. Many types of suicide are clearly highly irrational in this respect. For instance, suicides among schizophrenics are quite often based on bizarre beliefs about the nature of the world, and the methods employed in such cases can be equally bizarre. A schizophrenic may throw himself from a window believing that he will be transformed into a bird; this sort of suicide is irrational because it results from a world view that is very clearly false. . . .

The notion that rational suicide requires a realistic world view, however, raises difficulties concerning suicides based on strong religious convictions. . . . We are reluctant to call holders of these religious beliefs "irrational," even though no nonreligious evidence supports their beliefs. Consequently we find it difficult to term irrational a suicide performed in order to enter into this state. Similarly, it is difficult to label irrational a great variety of institutional suicides, even though the world view involved is different from our own. For instance, among certain African groups, at least according to

> *"Influenced . . . by television and cartoon figures who die but revive unharmed, children are not able to think of themselves as dead."*

James Frazer's famous account, it was common for kings to kill themselves or have themselves killed, either after a fixed term or at the first signs of debility, in order to promote their transformations into the next stages of divinity. The Scandinavian peoples practiced suicide in the belief that those who died by violence, rather than allowing themselves to succumb to sickness, age, or captivity, were assured of a place in Valhalla. Many primitive religions have held that an individual reaches the afterlife in the same condition in which he or she leaves this one; suicide is frequently practiced in these societies to avoid degenerative disease, senility, and so forth. Some religiously motivated suicides are irrational in the extreme, but, as H.J. Rose puts it,

> . . . religious suicides are not always maniacs . . . Nor can one justly class as maniacs those persons who hold that by killing themselves they can attain future happiness . . . or will return to life in this world stronger or wiser than before.

While suicide in these cases is similar to that of the psychotic, in that both are based on apparently unrealistic world views, it is clear that the rationality or irrationality of an individual's views of the world is relative to the environment in which he or she lives. We term the schizophrenic who thinks he can fly irrational because he has come to have this belief in a culture that offers no evidence for it; in the context of religious cultures, however, we do not usually label irrational those who adopt the views of the group, even if we believe them wrong. No doubt we take odd metaphysical beliefs as evidence of irrationality not because they are any more false than usual metaphysical beliefs, but because we suspect that the person who has odd beliefs, unlike his or her peers, has them because of some mental disability: He

> *"The notion that rational suicide requires a realistic world view . . . raises difficulties concerning suicides based on strong religious beliefs."*

or she has reacted in an abnormal way to the cultural dogmas of the society. This issue may, of course, raise larger questions of rationality and irrationality within cultural and religious systems, but it is important for our present examination because so much suicide is associated with it. In order that a suicide count as rational, it is only necessary that it be based on a world view that is consonant with the surrounding culture; we do not consider whether the world view of the culture as a whole is realistic or not. There may of course be considerable variation in world views within a culture; contemporary Western culture, for instance, includes both those whose view of the universe is materialistic and those whose view includes spiritual entities; neither sort of individual would be counted irrational in a suicide predicated upon such beliefs, though adherents of the opposite view would surely regard them as foolish.

Adequacy of Information

A rational action is performed not only in accordance with acceptable logical principles and based on a realistic world view, but is also based on adequate information. This third criterion is the basis of many claims that suicide can never be rational.

One quite poignant type of inadequately informed suicide is the person who reasons that if he has a painful terminal illness he will be better off to put an end to his life, and on the basis of a puzzled glance by his physician, or imagined but undiagnosed pains, wrongly assumes that he is dying. One of the Los Angeles suicide notes collected by Shneidman and Farberow reflects this sort of irrationality:

> Dearest Mary. This is to say goodbye. I have not told you because I did not want you to worry, but I have been feeling bad for 2 years, with my heart. I knew that if I went to a doctor I would lose my job. I think this is best for all concerned. I am in the car in the garage. Call the police but please don't come out there. I love you very much darling. Goodbye. Bill

A large number of similar cases, frequently involving fear of cancer, occur each year; in comparatively few of them is there any evidence of malignancy. An analogous type of case, also quite frequent, involves fear of pregnancy. . . .

The Avoidance of Harm

We also widely assume that an action, to be rational, must accord with the agent's own interests in the protection of his or her person and body from harm. For instance, self-mutilators strike us as irrational, since they cause themselves harm; suicides may strike us in the same way, since we assume that it is in one's own prudential interests to remain alive.

It may be argued, however, that death is not a harm to the individual who is dead. The process of painfully dying or knowing one is going to die, of course, can constitute an extraordinary harm, but once dead, the individual no longer exists, and therefore is no longer harmed. For this reason the prospective suicide, provided he or she selects a reasonably painless and expeditious method of carrying out a suicide plan, cannot be said to act contrary to his or her own prudential interests, since he or she does himself or herself no harm. In fact, R.M. Martin argues that even the suicide that is hastily planned, irrationally chosen, or undertaken for wholly inadequate reasons is not a harm to that individual, since that individual too is dead.

> The man who believes that death will bring him to paradise will not be disappointed; not because he will go to paradise, but because there won't be any him left after his death to be disappointed. Neither will the man who kills himself because he falsely believes he has a terminal disease regret his decision. The man who didn't know about therapy won't be worse off than he could have been had we intervened, after his suicide, since he won't exist at all. And the man who had the fleeting desire to kill himself and did won't suffer as a result of his desire's being only a fleeting one, as the man who went to live in the woods would.

. . . It is certainly clear that we count most harm-avoiding activities as rational. But this does not tell us whether harm-avoiding *suicides,* as distinguished from other harm-avoiding activities, can be considered rational. The answer depends in part on whether we consider death or suffering to be the greater evil. If death is the greater evil it is irrational to seek it, even if suffering can thereby be avoided; if, on the other hand, irremediable, relentless suffering is viewed as the worst thing that can befall a human being, then death undertaken to avoid it is not irrational. . . .

Accordance with Fundamental Interests

In general we regard an act as rational only if it is in accord with what we might call one's . . . basic interests, which themselves arise from one's most abiding, fundamental values. Sometimes these . . . fundamental interests are self-centered, in the sense that they are concerned with the acquisition or arrangement of things for the benefit of ourselves; sometimes, however, they are altruistic and concerned with the benefit of someone or something else. Thus an individual's [basic interests] may involve acquiring a bigger house, getting a better job, or learning various skills (though for some people such projects may be superficial ones only); they may also involve working for a cause, initiating reforms, or other projects of social improvement. They may even be malevolent; what is at immediate issue here is the rationality of an act, not its moral character.

An act that conflicts with the satisfaction of one's . . . fundamental goals is usually held to be irrational; an act intended to satisfy them is not. To put this another way, an act can be said to be rational in the sense that it is an effective means to a given end; the moral character of the end is not at issue. For instance, if a person has been working for years, say, for a liberal political cause, has attended party meetings and organized campaigns, but votes for the conservative candidate when there is no politically expedient reason to do so, we say that that person has acted irrationally; we would also say that he or she acts irrationally if he or she does not vote at all. In fact this person acts rationally only if he or she votes for the liberal candidate, since the success of the candidate is his or her goal. If a person has multiple but conflicting [basic goals], we will say that it is rational to act to satisfy the most basic of these. Suicide, since it ends life, appears to thwart the satisfaction of all of one's basic projects . . . , and so appears to be irrational in every case.

It is true that one cannot satisfy certain kinds of interests if one is dead, and the satisfaction of many [basic goals] requires the continuing existence of the agent. One cannot satisfy one's project to live in a bigger house if one does not live, nor can one perfect one's skills when dead. But not all [goals] require the continued existence of the agent: One's most important project may be essentially altruistic or centered on others, or may involve the furtherance of some valued institution or cause. So, for instance, parents whose fundamental goals include putting their children through college can have this [goal] satisfied, even if they are no longer alive. One's [goals] can sometimes even be satisfied if one kills oneself for them, as for instance in the parent who kills himself or herself in order to donate an organ and thus ensure the survival of his or her child. . . .

> *"If . . . relentless suffering is viewed as the worst thing that can befall a human being, then death undertaken to avoid it is not irrational."*

Of course suicide to accomplish a [goal] is rational only if that [goal] can be fulfilled regardless of whether one continues to exist or not. However, many [goals] we think of as independent of our own existence may not really be so. For instance, I may have dedicated my life to writing an article that could, in fact, be completed equally well by someone else; if so, the article is a [goal] that is independent of my own existence. If, for whatever reasons, my own suicide would implement the completion of this article (by somebody else), while my staying alive would impede it, it would not be irrational, at least on these grounds, to kill myself. But as John Perry says (working on his own article), "I want not merely that this article be completed, but that it be completed by me." Our involvement in even the most noble of projects often tends to be quite personal in this way, even though we are often unwilling or unable to admit it; but it is just this fact of personal involvement that precludes suicide as a rational choice in the accomplishment of that goal. . . .

In cases in which suicide, whether because it prevents harms, accomplishes goals, or expresses what is central to a human being, is a rational choice, is it always also rational to choose to remain alive? Is suicide, if it is rational in given circumstances, sometimes *the* rational choice, or is it always merely *a* rational choice among others? Clearly when strategies other than suicide will equally well prevent harms, accomplish goals, or express a person's deepest convictions, staying alive and using these other strategies will be at least an equally rational choice. But where other strategies will not succeed, suicide may be the only rational thing to do. This issue will have crucial practical consequences for the theory of rational suicide and the issue of rights.

> *"One cannot satisfy certain kinds of interests if one is dead."*

Suicide Violates
the Sanctity of Life

by William Murchison

About the author: *William Murchison is a nationally syndicated columnist for the* Dallas Morning News.

Among the many haunting and piteous images from the *Inferno* of Dante is this one. The travelers, in Canto XIII, enter a pathless wood. Dante, on Virgil's coaching, snaps a twig from a thorn tree.The tree yelps in pain, and no wonder. The tree is the transmuted personage of a formerly great Florentine, Pier delle Vigne, who had been counselor to the emperor Frederick II. How, then, did he become a tree? The envy of others brought him down. "Glad honours turned to obloquies" (as the Dorothy L. Sayers' translation would have it).

> So, in a scornful spirit of disgust,
> And thinking to escape from scorn by death,
> To my just self I made myself unjust.

Killed himself, in other words, by means unspecified here.

Miss Sayers expatiates in a footnote: "Accused of conspiring against his master, he was disgraced, imprisoned, and blinded, and in despair took his own life." Becoming, in consequence, a thorn tree, with leaves that Harpies loved to gnaw.

Again, Miss Sayers:

> The sin of Suicide is, in an especial manner, an insult to
> the body; so, here, the shades are deprived of even the
> semblance of the human form. As they refused life, they
> remain fixed in a dead and withered sterility. They are
> the image of the self-hatred which dries up the very sap
> of energy and makes all life infertile.

Would you say there is a problem here? Most moderns likely would. The theological strictures against suicide are easy enough, perhaps, to defend in the abstract. Then the Wood of the Suicides heaves into view, and there is the thorn tree known in the day of sunshine and honor as Pier delle Vigne. Disgraced,

Reprinted from "The Dark, Dark Wood of Suicide," by William Murchison, *Chronicles,* August 1998. Reprinted with permission.

abandoned, blinded: Well, naturally he killed himself! Why not? The temptation to say so is immense and, may I add, understandable in everyday, ordinary human terms. That the pitiful Pier, by ending his worldly sufferings, brought himself pains far worse is, shall we say, a hard sell in the Age of Empathy.

The tug of war between suffering and escape persists throughout literature and history. Here is Kipling, just a century ago, counseling "the young British soldier":

> When you're wounded and left on Afghanistan's plains,
> And the women come 'round to cut up what remains
> Just roll to your rifle and blow out your brains
> And go to your Gawd like a soldier.

With never a thought for thorn trees, the poet might have added.

Assisted Suicide

The rise of the "assisted" suicide movement, pushing itself up like a weed patch through the manicured grass of the old moral-religious order, lays these matters urgently before us. Dr. Jack Kevorkian's "patients" claim the right to end their sufferings. Oregon has lately ratified that desire. It cannot end here. Why accord the terminally ill rights superior to those enjoyed by the merely despondent or world-weary? Under the Oregon dispensation, poor Pier delle Vigne could not have obtained permission to take himself off.

Even worse is indicated—the general embrace of euthanasia, as forecast in the 70's and 80's by such as Malcolm Muggeridge and Walker Percy. No, no, no! object the proponents of suicide. Never that! Personal autonomy is all they seek: the right, not the duty, to die.

We have a saying in the South: that ol' dog won't hunt. This dog won't either.

To see why, we need to revisit medieval Florence for a brief inspection of its foundations. Those foundations, on which Dante walked, and yes, Pier delle Vigne and Frederick II, were religious—specifically, Christian. The earth was the Lord's and the fullness thereof (as the psalmist said). Into that fullness human bodies and souls were incorporated.

Pier delle Vigne's body, though he might inhabit it, was not his own; it belonged, rather, to God. The malign and cruel things that others did to Pier were thus the business of God, who was certain, in response, to do two things: bless Pier with the release of death—if not necessarily on Pier's timetable—and bring retribution on his persecutors. Pier's suicide, for whatever poignant reasons, disturbed the divine symmetry of mercy and justice. Off he went to the dark wood, to bleed and cry out.

Very well; it was at best a long time ago, and as we all know, the *Divine Comedy* is a great work of the imagination. Even before the deconstructionist age, we knew Dante didn't *actually* enter some "rough and stubborn forest" alongside a dead Roman poet. What has all this to do with the price of eggs in Arkansas? Only everything, I would venture.

Life Belongs to God

The Pier delle Vigne story takes us, shakes us, wakes us. In it we see—ourselves. Any of us, in the same position, *might* have done as did the old Florentine. But this is the merest starting place. The delle Vigne story points up, it seems to me, at least two essential considerations. First, life is a religious proposition. Which, of course, it has to be if God initiated it. Not that moderns are automatically persuaded of this view, which seems not to square, as the irrepressible Episcopal Bishop John Spong recently put it, with post-Darwinian reality. The interesting thing is, there are no full-blown alternative explanations—certainly none that invest life with objective value. The Darwinian view in fact exalts destruction and displacement. Move over! Get out of the way!

The value of human life, in God's eyes, is one of Dante's subtexts. If life lacked objective value, Dante would hardly make so big a deal of divine justice—the meting out of reward or punishment in line with how particular lives are used. The assumption of divine sovereignty, as differently as different times and places spin that assumption, provides a comprehensive understanding.

Second, the religious view is absolutely, totally, 100 percent indispensable in understanding who man is and—in the context of our present discussion—what he must do. I make this claim with no deference whatever to, shall we say, secular viewpoints. These viewpoints are as useless as a map of Bombay if you're lost in Florence, trying to find the Duomo.

If the religious view enjoys nowhere near the dominance characteristic of Dante's time, that makes it urgent to recover such a view. Look where we are otherwise: lost in a dark wood; unsure where the road is leading. The suicide question is ideal for framing this discussion.

The question, save perhaps in deconstructionist circles, is not: Did this poor old man, Pier delle Vigne, *deserve* to become a thorn tree, just because he was tired and in pain? The question is: Where does authority over life properly reside, with the Potter or His vessel?

> *"Pier delle Vigne's body, though he might inhabit it, was not his own; it belonged, rather, to God."*

To come down on the side of Pier is to decouple theology and justice. Justice becomes what *we* make of it, in our human searchings and musings, our cross-questionings and re-examinations. The opportunities this affords! Against the backdrop of the "assisted suicide" drama, these opportunities appear in plain relief. The principal actor on the stage is the sufferer, whose suffering no one in the audience doubts for a minute. Lonely, wracked by pain, he cries out for release. Eyes moisten. Who could refuse him? As for rumors of eternal punishment . . . forget such ahistorical and speculative rubbish!

What Dorothy Sayers calls "the intimate and unbreakable bond between spirit and flesh" is of scant interest to a secularized society like our own. Bond, what bond? Ending pain is what counts. And beyond the body's escape—its flight from pain? Here the matter truly breaks down. There exists no "beyond" that anyone is obliged to note. We do not run our open, democratic, pluralistic society on religious principle, you know.

Indeed, we do not: not since the 60's anyway. We run society on another principle entirely—the principle that no one principle is better than another one. We call it pluralism: everybody-for-himselfism. If Joe Dokes, counselor to the President, has been pulled down by envy and jailed by the independent prosecutor and thoroughly ruined and wants in consequence to end it all . . . well, who can object? Surely it is for Joe to decide whether he would live or die.

And "the intimate and unbreakable bond between spirit and flesh"? Dear, dear, certainly can't judge that one! Some say yes, some say no. Officially the United States of America is . . . in agreement with both sides. Vast are the consequences of this agreement—topped by the deterioration of the old sense that human life is special; so special that the discarding of it, in pain and despair, outrages some immemorial covenant between donor and recipient.

> *"Abortion [can lead] to assisted suicide, assisted suicide to euthanasia as sensibilities go to sleep and mental resistance crumbles."*

The so-called slippery slope argument is oversimplified: that is, by allowing "A" we find demand rising for "B," which takes us to "C," smack dab on the superhighway to "D."

"A" most certainly can lead to "B": abortion to assisted suicide, assisted suicide to euthanasia as sensibilities go to sleep and mental resistance crumbles. This skirts, even so, a still larger point—that the erosion of belief in the divine sanction for life makes it *all* possible, and likely much more. Suicide is far from the whole of the matter. Indifference to life takes varied forms, including that of a teenager, armed with hunting rifle and pistol, calmly picking off his schoolmates.

The Big Picture

"Pluralism," the modern deity, has made it impolite to tout a religious sanction for life. Yet what other sanctions exist? Well, laws, to be sure; but laws can be changed, as were the abortion laws by Supreme Court fiat. Laws depend on the convictions of those who choose the lawmakers. At present, those convictions are considerably shaped by the slap-happy secular model—you do your thing, I'll do mine; and, oh, yes, I do feel, in my inner self, your pain. By whatever route we fetched up at the bottom of this slope, no safe footing is to be found there. The old premise—life is good—washes much more poorly than it once did. "Consumer choice" increasingly becomes the determinant.

The question is much larger than suicide. Suicide is a corner of the picture:

one response to the perception that the body belongs to its tenant and nobody better tell him how to use it, see?

Kevorkian today, Auschwitz tomorrow? That is one way of looking at it, and not the worst way by any means. (In *The Thanatos Syndrome,* Walker Percy does look at it so.) Just from the daily news we find that suicide has become in many instances an escape route not from pain but from responsibility.

> **"Kevorkian today, Auschwitz tomorrow?"**

I write these lines in the week a Florida man suspected of murdering his four-year-old son overpowered two policemen taking him to jail, shot them both to death, murdered a state trooper—and committed suicide. His indifference to human life was total: other's lives, his own life. As deftly as he might have chosen a Ford Taurus over a Geo, Fritos over Lays potato chips, our alienated consumer elected death over life. Next day, a 15-year-old boy, suspended from school for carrying a gun, barged into the high school cafeteria, firing his rifle as he went. "It didn't look like he was bothered by anything," a student said. "Like the shooting was just something he was doing."

Taking a Religious Stance

In the 90's a religious stance is forbidden society? We cannot officially bury our pain and passions in piety toward the Creator of life? If not, we are in vast trouble. We need—promptly, decisively—to change. The religious view of life—its origins, its destinations—urgently needs resuscitation. Suicide as an imputed 20th-century "right"—on a par with trial by jury—would be a laughable concept, save that nothing about it is funny.

Poor Pier delle Vigne! Poor old thorn tree! Was he so terribly disadvantaged at that? Amid undeserved suffering he had one resource no enemy arrow could penetrate, no branding iron could scorch—the love and mercy of God. This he discarded. In the religious view—the Christian view that supposedly informed Pier and his contemporaries—earthly misery is no barrier to joy. If anything, according to that worldview, misery functions as a ladder, boosting the sufferer higher, higher, and so at last over the heavenly fence. Always provided he remains faithful—as Pier did not.

High on the list of diseases afflicting candidates for assisted suicide is amyotrophic lateral sclerosis—Lou Gehrig's disease; a truly awful way to die, marked by progressive paralysis of basic physical functions, including, at the last, breathing. Life with ALS can hardly be described as life at all.

Except that, in a case with which I am familiar—the case of a young traditionalist Episcopal priest with a ministry to Washington, D.C.'s, inner-city children—ALS proved a vehicle for heroism and inspiration. The priest and his family offered his suffering to God for whatever use the Creator of the Universe might make of it. He must have found it useful indeed. Happiness flooded the afflicted family: joy at serving the Lord and at awaiting His pleasure. That pleasure, the Lord had made known in the hearts of the afflicted, embraced ever so much more than the hospital bed on which his suffering servant lay. When the end finally came, it was not—how shall I put this?—the end. It was the beginning.

Such things are easy enough to say, I suppose, from the outside looking in. One should not draw unduly large deductions from someone else's sufferings. But, then, suffering is part of life. Unable to abolish it, we may indeed settle contentedly for escape. But there is another alternative: dealing with suffering, directly and forcefully; turning evil—it comes down to this—into good.

Can a secular world be made to see such things? Well, the world, before it was secular, saw such things with relative clarity. Whether it understood them perfectly or not, it drank them in with humility. Hearts might ooze blood in behalf of Pier delle Vigne; but as to the fitness of his punishment—that was just how things were. And had to be.

Neither "pluralism" nor the semi-paganism so fashionable today is an excuse for the refusal to assert the theological value of life. A defense of life on secular premises can be mounted—yes, of course. But these premises, as we see, are slender and weak. They collapse when stepped on hard, as with abortion and maybe also, quite soon, with euthanasia. Human will, human selfishness, human pride do the stepping. We're modern! What we want, we get! Or else.

Amid his thorny branches in the dark, dark wood, what must poor old Mr. delle Vigne be thinking?

The Bible Does Not Tolerate Suicide

by Robert Barry

About the author: *Robert Barry is a biblical scholar.*

Professor Margaret Battin has claimed that the Bible contains no explicit condemnations of suicide and that the Bible not only tolerated self-killing but also positively encouraged it. Similar sentiments were recently declared by the Ninth Circuit Court of Appeals in *Compassion in Dying v. Washington* where the Court states: "The stories of four suicides are noted in the Old Testament—Sampson, Saul, Abimlech [sic], and Achitophel—and none is treated as an act worthy of censure. In the New Testament, the suicide of Judas Iscariot is not treated as a further sin, rather as an act of repentance." But this view cannot go unchallenged, as it manifests a superficial and unreflective understanding of biblical material. This view fails to see that Scripture condemns or approves of actions in many different ways. Professor Battin asserts that the prohibition of killing in the Decalogue does not prohibit suicide but only murder. But *Genesis* 9:6 forbade the shedding of innocent blood by anyone and did not explicitly exclude reflexively lethal acts: "He who sheds man's blood, shall have his blood shed by man, for in the image of God man was made." This injunction was purposely general, for it condemned the shedding of blood, be it one's own or another's, and the only instance in which the Bible allowed killing was either for self-defense or for the purpose of punishing an individual for a clear and certain serious breach of the law. This prohibition was carried rather far by some in ancient Judaism for they would execute by stoning to avoid shedding blood. The fundamental reason for this was that innocent human life was not to be destroyed because it was made in the image of God, but Battin discounts this principle and fails to analyze the concept of *imago Dei* [the image of God].

Exodus 23:7 condemned killing of the *innocent:* "The innocent and just person you shall not put to death," which Professor Battin regards as applying only to homicide. But this law has usually been understood to mean that no one

Excerpted from "The Biblical Teachings on Suicide," by Robert Barry, *Issues in Law and Medicine,* Winter 1997. Reprinted with permission.

should be killed who does not deserve to die, including oneself. Relative to modern law and morality, the Israelite law on killing was primitive, and by itself, is not able to stand as an adequate moral norm today. Early Israelite laws held that guilt should be presumed if there was known enmity between the killer and victim. Just as the biblical teaching that adulterers should be stoned may be considered harsh and ineffective, so also its precepts on killing may be considered not fully developed. The important point is that these laws were correct in condemning these actions as immoral, but the punishments to be meted out for them were unduly harsh because of the roughness and insensibility of the Israelites at the time. The Decalogue condemned willful killing of the innocent, but this judgment was not as refined as it should be. And even though the Decalogue clearly prohibited destroying innocent human life, it did not precisely define the object of the culpably lethal action.

> *"The suicide of Judas Iscariot is not treated as a further sin, rather as an act of repentance."*

In order to fully understand the biblical vision of suicide, one must also see how death was understood. In general, the Old Testament saw death as a tragic condition because it condemned the person to the darkness of Sheol where they experienced mere existence and little else. This tradition interprets the Genesis creation story to mean that humanity was not created to die, but rather that death came as a result of the primeval offense of Adam and Eve, a view reaffirmed in *Sirach* 25:24. Death was not seen as trivial or frivolous and there was a proper dread of death, for *Psalms* 49:16–17 expressed hope in Yahweh for delivery from it. Elsewhere, an extremely pessimistic view of death was expressed. Koheleth declared: "For the fate of the sons of men and the fate of the beasts is the same; as one dies so dies the other. They all have the same breath, and man has no advantage over the beasts; for all is vanity." The bleakness of our existence continues after death when "there is no work or thought or knowledge or wisdom in Sheol, to which you are going," and by "a living dog is better than a dead lion," he reminds his readers that he who is living has "hope." Consciousness and our awareness of our dying is the basis of the majesty of the human person, and the nobility of the person who is dying is that they are aware they are dying. "For the living know that they will die, but the dead know nothing. . . ." The only desirable death was at the end of a long and happy life lived securely in Israel which took place in the midst of one's family with the fullness of powers still intact. The opposite was a long and slow death after a long illness because it embittered.

In the New Testament, sin was seen as the cause of death. Paul explicitly held that all die in Adam but will rise in Christ, and death was the last adversary of Christ. Christ robbed death of its power which made Him Lord of life, and having risen from the dead, death was powerless over Him. The Christian will experience victory over death by sharing in the death of Christ in this life, and in this, the "old person" is crucified and the "new person" raised up with Him. Faith in Christ does not protect from death in this life, but gave hope that one would not suffer death eternally.

There are two perspectives on suicide in the Old Testament. On the one hand, there were suicides that were condemned in various ways, but on the other hand a few were tolerated because they expressed extraordinary devotion to God such as that of Samson and Razis. These deaths were tolerated more as martyrdoms than as suicides. But whenever anyone requested to be killed by God, this was clearly and explicitly refused and this divine verdict goes to the heart of the biblical teachings on suicide. By denying any such requests, God declared the immorality of suicide and set an example for all people: suicide was not to be done for any reason, either for selfless or selfish reasons.

In spite of what Professor Battin claims, the classical view that the biblical materials condemn suicide can be sustained, and in the following sections, I will review episodes involving suicide in the Scriptures to show that the Bible does not approve of or condone, but in fact condemns self-killing.

Suicides Sought, but Refused by Yahweh

The appeals made by some in the Bible to God to be killed are important for determining the biblical view on suicide. In each case, an individual begs for death, in essence making a suicidal gesture, and his plea is always denied by God. These cases show that while the human verdict about suicide might be ambiguous in some instances, the divine verdict is quite clear. If suicide was as unobjectionable in the Bible as Professor Battin contends, then one would expect Yahweh in his compassion and mercy to allow his faithful and beloved ones to kill themselves because of frustrated devotion. Instead Yahweh turns a deaf ear to appeals for suicides, as if to say that suicide is not an option, even for his most faithful ones. Not only does He not allow his faithful ones to destroy themselves, but He also condemns sinners who do this.

> *"The only instance in which the Bible allowed killing was either for self-defense or for . . . punishing an individual for . . . a break of the law."*

Moses. Even one so great as Moses was tempted to suicide. After the Israelites fled slavery in Egypt, one day in the desert they stood weeping and whining about being taken from Egypt. Moses became so disillusioned with the Israelites that he retreated to his tent in despair and frustration and pleaded with Yahweh to simply end his life:

Moses heard the people weeping, each family at the door of his tent. Yahweh's anger was greatly aroused; Moses too found it disgraceful, and he said to Yahweh: 'Why do you treat your servant so badly? In what respect have I failed to win your favor, for you to lay the burden of all these people on me? Was it I who conceived all these people, was I their father, for you to say to me, "Carry them in your arms, like a foster-father carrying around an unweaned child, to the country which I swore to give their fathers?" Where am I to find meat to give all these people, pestering me with their tears and saying, "Give us meat to eat?" I cannot carry all these people on my own; the weight is too much for me. If this is how you mean to treat me, please kill me outright!'

In response to Moses' plea, Yahweh did not kill him or allow him to commit suicide, but rather assembled the elders of the community, conferred a portion of his Spirit on them, and sent them quail. In fact he would give them so much meat to eat it would "come out of their nostrils and sicken you!" The message of this story is clearly that God does not turn a deaf ear to our needs, but grants them in abundance to those who were patient and waited for him. . . .

> *"Consciousness and our awareness of our dying is the basis of the majesty of the human person."*

Jonah. The story of Jonah is the best example of God refusing to condone suicide. Jonah was a reluctant prophet who was called to preach repentance to Nineveh at a time when the Israelites detested the Assyrians. The story tells of the universalism of divine mercy and forgiveness and of God's desire to give life and help to all. But rather than heeding Yahweh's call to preach repentance to the Ninevites, Jonah boarded a ship headed in the opposite direction, and when he was in danger of drowning, a giant fish was sent by Yahweh to save his life. When he finally made it to Nineveh and preached a message of repentance, the Ninevites bitterly disappointed him by repenting. Jonah then went outside the city and sulked under a vine hoping that the Ninevites would be punished, and asked Yahweh for death. . . .

From the perspective of the morality of suicide, Yahweh did not grant permission for suicide for any reason, either for the altruistic reasons of Elijah or the selfish and egotistical reasons of Jonah. He does not want to bring death to Moses, Nineveh, Elijah or Jonah, but wanted all to live. He will even show this desire to give life to all by using nature to save them, for the crows fed Elijah and the whale saved Jonah. . . .

Suicides Countenanced in the Old Testament

Samson. The story of Samson was one of an amoral giant with uncontrollable anger and lust who waged a war of private revenge against the Philistines. He was a unique figure with little religious aura, and his feats reached extravagant proportions because he was the only one of his time who could give the Israelites hope when they were wholly dominated by the Philistines. Samson betrayed Yahweh by falling into illicit relationships with Philistine women and this infidelity sapped his strength. He died in an attempt to avenge and punish the Philistines for their irreverence and oppression of the Israelites. But he was able to bring death on them because his strength was restored after he was blinded and then pledged his loyalty and obedience to Yahweh again. . . .

Augustine and Aquinas argued that Samson's suicide was a morally valid killing done under a divine command, and this may have been true. But Samson may have actually been directly intending to kill the Philistines under a divine command and only indirectly kill himself. Rather than committing suicide, he may have been directly intending to punish the Philistines for their blasphemy and also sacrifice himself as a martyr in punishment for his own infidelity. Samson's death had a double meaning, for it was a sign that Yahweh's favor and power had been restored through the destruction of his enemies and it also signified Yahweh's punishment of Samson for his infidelity. The purpose of his death was not to show that suicide was justified in some instances, but that his self-sacrifice restored him to favor with Yahweh. His death showed that he loved God so perfectly that he was willing to die for Him. . . .

Suicides Condemned in the Bible

Saul. The other type of suicide in the Old Testament was performed by those who were utterly alienated from God, and these suicides were a sign not of devotion and loyalty to God, but of total alienation from Him. These individuals committed suicide because they alienated themselves from divine favor by violating a grave religious duty and the evil they performed recoiled on their heads in the form of suicide. The Scriptures do not explicitly and formally declare suicide to be against the law of God, but they do portray those who deliberately killed themselves without his authority to be alienated from the life and holiness of God.

Saul violated his divine consecration and was punished for this by a rebellion in his kingdom. He was specifically anointed by Yahweh to be the great king and unifier of the Chosen People, but he betrayed his mission by falling into sorcery, idolatry, and witchcraft. For this, he slowly became entangled in the snares of sin, infidelity and death until he was so deeply enmeshed that he could not escape, and the depths of his involvement was confirmed by his self-killing. His life and actions were in sharp contrast to the scriptural ideal of the God-fearing Israelite who lived out the full length of his days and saw his children's children down to the seventh generation. Saul was driven to desperation and was finally forced to kill himself. . . .

> *"Whenever anyone requested to be killed by God, this was clearly and explicitly refused."*

Professor Battin claims that the scriptural author simply reports the suicide of Saul without any comment that would either condemn or approve it, but that is hardly true. Saul's body was beheaded and his corpse nailed to a city wall. His armor was placed in the temple of a Philistine idol and his memory mocked. And rather than being reverently buried, his remains were burned, an act of desecration of remains seldom done to an Israelite. This extraordinary humiliation and desecration was condemnation of his suicide in a biblical style, for his death was not glorified as was Samson's or Razis'. Rather than being greeted with mourning, his life was treated as a profound disgrace and those who buried him fasted, an appropriate action as a penance for sin. It can hardly be said that his action was countenanced by the devout of the time. . . .

> *"While the human verdict about suicide might be ambiguous in some instances, the divine verdict is quite clear."*

Judas Iscariot. The suicide of Judas Iscariot illustrates the New Testament's critical view of this act, for he committed suicide in imitation of Ahithophel and apparently was his New Testament counterpart. By committing suicide just prior to the death of Jesus, Judas ironically proclaimed Him to be in the line of the Davidic kingship, just as the suicide of Ahithophel ironically proclaimed the kingship of David. Judas was chosen to be a member of the apostolic community by Jesus, and he was given privileged intimacy and knowledge of the Lord because of that call. But Judas rejected this call and betrayed Jesus. Because of this he was denied not only knowledge of the Resurrected Lord, but he was also shunned by the community and the Christian tradition has long held that he was the only one certainly excluded from the kingdom because he did not repent of his suicide. . . .

In the Bible, God never accepted pleas for suicide or to kill out of compassion. The suicides of Saul, Ahitophel, Zimri, Judas and Abimelech were not extolled but denounced as a punishment for the evil of one's life, they were the evil of one's sin "recoiling on one's head." Whether the pleadings were from faithful and zealous servants of Yahweh such as Moses, Elijah, Sarah or Job, or pleas from the selfish such as Jonah, they were not countenanced. The *martyrdoms* of Samson and Razis were tolerated only because they expressed astonishing devotion to the Law and will of God. In the New Testament, Paul shows convincingly that the appropriate Christian response to those tempted to suicide is to heed the call of the Apostles and place one's faith in Jesus Christ. It can hardly be said that suicide is tolerated or accepted in the Bible, for the sacrifice of one's life is only accepted if it is a means of serving God.

Suicide Is Not a Rational Act

by Bijou Yang and David Lester

About the authors: *Bijou Yang is a professor of economics at Drexel University, Philadelphia; David Lester is a professor of psychology at the Richard Stockton College of New Jersey. Lester has written over fifty books and over one thousand articles on suicide and murder.*

The present viewpoint reviews several recent analyses of suicidal behaviour which continue the growing tradition of applying economic models to non-economic behaviour. [It] describes a cost-benefit analysis and a demand-supply analysis of suicidal behaviour, with implications for preventing suicide. . . .

An Economic Model for Suicide

In most economic models for suicide, committing suicide is considered to be a rational act. An individual is acting 'rationally' if, given a choice between various alternatives, he or she selects what seems to be the most desirable or least undesirable alternative. Thus, from this perspective, suicide can be a rational act. None the less, economists do not judge whether suicide is wrong, immoral or a deviant act.

Costs and benefits: Applying traditional economic marginal analysis to suicidal behaviour, [in a 1987 study B.Y. Yeh and Lester] suggested that the decision to commit suicide depends upon the benefits and costs associated with suicide. An individual will be less likely to commit suicide if the benefits from suicide decrease, the costs of suicide increase, the costs of alternative actions decrease, or the benefits from alternative activities increase.

The benefits from suicide include escape from physical or psychological pain (as in the suicide of someone dying from terminal cancer), the anticipation of the impact of the suicide's death on other people (as in someone who hopes to make the survivors feel guilty), or restoring one's public image (as in the suicide of Antigone—in Sophocles's play of the same name). In addition, the act itself may be enjoyable. Those who self-injure themselves by cutting their

Excerpted from "Conceptualizing Suicide in Economic Models," by Bijou Yang and David Lester, *Applied Economics Letters*, vol. 3, 1996. Reprinted with permission from Taylor & Francis, Ltd. Article available at www.tandf.co.uk/journals.

wrists sometimes report that the act of cutting relieves built-up tension and that they feel no pain.

There are several costs in committing suicide. These include the money and effort spent in obtaining the information and equipment needed for the act of suicide, the pain involved in preparing to kill oneself and in the process of committing suicide, the expected loss as a result of committing suicide such as the expected punishment predicted by most of the major religions of the world, and the opportunity costs (that is, the net gain to be expected if other alternative activities were chosen and life continued).

From this perspective, an individual will engage in suicidal behaviour only if its benefits are greater than all of the costs mentioned above. Therefore, our economic model would suggest that suicide could be prevented by increasing its costs or by decreasing its benefits.

A demand and supply analysis of suicide: Let us assume that suicide is a commodity or service that we purchase. It is obvious that suicide is very different from the typical objects that we purchase. For example, when we buy an object, we pay a specific price to obtain it and then we enjoy it. Suicide results in death, and as a result we have to conceptualize our enjoyment of it quite differently. (Suicide is somewhat similar to the purchasing of health care services. In both, we pay a price to get rid of something, life in the case of suicide and sickness in the case of health care. Yet there is a basic difference between suicide and health care in that suicide leads to death while it is hoped that health care leads to further life. Of course, for those who believe that there will be a 'life-after-death', suicide also leads to further life, but of a different kind.)

Looking at matters from a demand-side perspective, when we purchase a commodity (or a service), the price we pay for the commodity (or service) reflects the benefits we expect to receive from consuming that commodity. From a demand-side perspective, beef costs more than chicken because the public desires beef more, and their stronger desire for beef reflects their expectation of greater satisfaction from eating beef than from eating chicken.

In the demand-side analysis of suicide, the notion of its 'price' is different from the ordinary price of a commodity. The benefit expected by a suicide is the relief of tremendous distress. Accordingly, we must use a scale of distress to measure the benefit expected by the suicidal individual. This benefit expected by the suicidal individual is reflected in the price he must pay for his suicide.

> *"The decision to commit suicide depends upon the benefits and costs associated with suicide."*

Accordingly, the demand curve is a relationship indicating the probability of committing suicide as a function of the amount of distress felt by the individual. As the amount of distress increases, the probability of committing suicide increases. The demand for suicide is, therefore, an upward sloping curve, which is quite different from the typical downward sloping demand curve found in most economic analyses.

The Cost of Suicide

On the supply side, the probability of committing suicide is related to the cost of committing suicide. The cost of committing suicide includes the cost of losing your life, collecting information about how to commit the act, purchasing the means for suicide, etc. While the latter two items have a clear-cut scale of measurement, the cost of losing life is much harder to measure. It includes at least three components, namely, the psychological fear of death, the loss of income over the future which otherwise would have been earned by the suicide, and the loss of any enjoyment that would be experienced during the rest of your 'normal' life.

The higher the cost of committing suicide, the lower the probability that an individual would actually commit suicide. Therefore, the supply curve should be a downward sloping curve.

It is important in such a demand-supply analysis of suicide to convert the psychological variables (level of distress and future pleasure) into measures comparable to monetary unit, so that an equilibrium can be obtained through equating the demand and supply for suicide. One way to measure the level of distress is to operationalize it as the cost of the psychological services required to eliminate the distress that the suicidal person is experiencing. Since there is a typical price for psychological services, each level of distress could be converted into a monetary measure representing the cost of psychological services needed to eliminate the distress. This is complicated by the fact that psychological services are not always effective. Some people do not benefit from treatment. This could be taken into account by incorporating the probability of success of the treatment into the calculations, as a multiplier of the cost of treatment. Converting future pleasure from life into monetary units is more difficult. One alternative could be to convert all of the components of the cost into subjective units, based on the ratings given by representative members of society.

> *"The higher the cost of committing suicide, the lower the probability that an individual would actually commit suicide."*

Factors behind the supply and demand for suicide: [In their 1987 study Yeh and Lester] examined some of the factors which contributed to the decision to commit suicide based on a [1983] review of the literature of suicide by Lester. They noted that most of the factors, such as psychiatric disturbance, gender and age, and dysfunctional families of origin, are reasonably stable characteristics. Thus, once the demand curve is formed, it will remain quite stable over time. Sudden shifts in the demand curve might be caused by events such as sudden deaths of significant others, illness or work difficulties, but the extent of the shifts in the demand curve as a result of these factors may be quite limited.

Labour-Force Analogies

[In a 1991 paper, W.C.] Huang applied economic analyses of the decision to enter and leave the labour market to suicidal behaviour conceptualized as a decision to enter or leave the 'life market'. The decision to leave the life market will be based on maximizing utility. The utility, according to Huang, will encompass more than income, including as well as dimensions of the worth or value of life, such as love, health, fame, beauty, fun, adventure, prestige, respect, security, etc. This life income has to be earned, and it is a struggle to gain some of these rewards. Obtaining them requires a great deal of hard 'labour' (L).

The opposite of work is leisure, rest and relaxation (R). Leisure entails letting go of pressure and responsibility. The maximum manifestation of leisure is complete and permanent rest—death. Labour measures the extent of effort and resolve to live while leisure measures its lack. The expected wage of market rate (W) is the perceived opportunity of ability to earn life income for a unit of life effort.

Two solutions are possible. Most people will choose an interior solution, choosing to live with a varying amount of effort. Some will be unable to find an interior solution, and they may choose to drop out of the life market, that is, commit suicide, analogously to discouraged workers dropping out of the labour market.

People will decide to drop out of the life market if the perceived obtainable wage in the life market falls short of some minimally acceptable level, perhaps as a result of a terminal disease, recurring depressions, business fiascos, public humiliation, etc. Less probably, the decision to commit suicide can also be caused by an increase in the reservation wage. For an individual wealthy in the sense of life, he or she may need more to keep life interesting and challenging. Having so much of everything, his utility from life diminishes and he may become tired of life. Given a much higher reservation

> *"Sudden shifts in the demand curve [of suicide] might be caused by events such as sudden deaths of significant others, illness or work difficulties."*

wage than the average person, and without a matched increase in perceived wage, the individual may find the corner solution desirable and choose to commit suicide.

Huang noted that, in this perspective, suicide is not irrational. However, suicide may not be the correct solution, especially because of the uncertainty of the future. Life market information is always incomplete and imperfect. In the model W was the *perceived* expected wage from living, and the individual's perception may be erroneous.

Economists define rational behaviour as maximizing some variable such as utility of profit. [In his 1962 study, 'Irrational Behaviour and Economic Theory,' G.S.] Becker defined two types of irrational behaviour: (1) random, erratic and whimsical choices and (2) perseverative choices in which the person chooses what he or she has always chosen in the past. [In our 1991 response to Becker's paper, we] argued that these two types of irrational behaviour paralleled the major typology of suicidal behaviour in which suicidal behaviour is seen as a time-limited impulsive crisis or as a chronic maladaptive pattern. . . .

Suicide Attempts as Signalling Games

[R.W. Rosenthal, in the 1993 study 'Suicide Attempts and Signalling Games,'] focused on suicide attempts which have chances of either success or failure (that is, suicide attempts of moderate to severe severity, where the individual is 'gambling' with the outcome). He suggested that the suicide attempt can be seen as a signal intended to manipulate the receiver's behaviour in a way favourable to the sender. In this respect, it resembles a game.

In this perspective, the sender may be either depressed or normal, and it

> *"The maximum manifestation of leisure is complete and permanent rest—death."*

is assumed that the players know the respective probabilities of these two possibilities. The sender knows his type while the receiver does not. The sender chooses an attempt (signal) strength (which determines whether he or she survives). The receiver then chooses a sympathetic or unsympathetic response. The receiver would prefer to respond sympathetically to a depressed sender and unsympathetically to a normal sender. Both types of sender would prefer a sympathetic response, but the preference is stronger in the depressed sender.

Rosenthal's . . . analysis suggested two hypotheses. First, gambling-type suicidal behaviour would be less common if the suicidal individual strongly demanded a sympathetic response. Second, if the receiver is very likely to give a sympathetic response, then depressed senders are less likely to engage in gambling-type suicidal behaviour.

Suicide as an Investment Under Uncertainty

[In their 1994 book *Investment Under Uncertainty*, A.K. Dixit and R.S. Pindyck] examined the nature of investment under conditions of uncertainty. Although their book focused on the investment decisions of firms, they noted that other decisions are made with the same conditions as investments: the decision is irreversible, there is uncertainty over the future rewards of the decision, and there is some leeway over the timing of the decision.

Dixit and Pindyck noted that suicide fits these criteria. They noted that [D.S. Hamermesh and N. Soss, in their 1974 study 'An Economic Theory of Suicide,'] had argued that an individual will commit suicide when the expected value of the utility of the rest of his or her life falls short of some benchmark (or down to zero). . . . Suicide is irreversible, and the future is quite uncertain. Therefore, the option of waiting to see if the situation improves should be a likely choice. Even if the expected direction of life is downward, there may still be some non-zero positive probability that it will improve.

Dixit and Pindyck speculated that suicides project the bleak present into an equally bleak future. They ignore the uncertainty of the future and the option value of life. In this respect, Dixit and Pindyck saw suicides as irrational.

They argued that religious and moral proscriptions against suicide compensate to some extent for this failure of rationality. These proscriptions raise the perceived cost of suicide and lower the threshold of the quality of life that precipitates suicide. . . .

Preventing Suicide

These perspectives . . . have implications for the prevention of suicide. For example, it was noted that a simple application of an economic demand and supply model to suicidal behaviour provided a justification for particular strategies for suicide prevention, such as the establishment of suicide prevention services. Rosenthal's signalling game analogy also has implications for suicide prevention. If the receiver is likely to give a sympathetic response, then depressed senders are less likely to engage in gambling-type suicidal behaviour. Thus, friends and relatives of potentially suicidal individuals should be encouraged to give sympathetic responses, and many suicide education programs given to high school students train the students to respond in sympathetic ways to their suicidal peers.

In the investment under uncertainty perspective, suicidal people extrapolate from a grim present to the future, and ignore the uncertainty of the future. Thus, counselling techniques which challenge this pessimistic point of view and reduce the hopelessness of the individual should prove effective.

Chapter 2

What Are the Causes of Suicide?

Theories of Suicide: An Overview

by Paul R. Robbins

About the author: *Paul R. Robbins is the author of* Adolescent Suicide *as well as other books on health and psychology.*

Why do people commit suicide? This is a very difficult question to answer, for suicide flies in the face of what we see throughout the multitudinous forms of life that exist on this planet, where the impetus toward survival seems fundamental. One has only to look at nature films on a public television channel to witness the struggles that animals make to hang onto life. Yet people kill themselves, and young people who seemingly have the richest, most fulfilling part of their lives ahead of them are not immune from self-destruction.

When we ask for explanations for suicide, we are in a real sense asking for theories, for the question *why do people kill themselves?* is far from settled. A theory states what someone believes might be happening. If a theory is useful, it can suggest avenues for research that investigators can pursue. A theory provides a guide for where to look and what to study. When a theory is carefully formulated, it can be tested by research to see how valid it is. If the data support the theory, fine. If not, the theory may have to be modified or even discarded. This is, of course, the way of science. Theories and explanations for suicidal behavior have been proposed from several academic disciplines—sociology, psychiatry and psychology, and biology. These explanations offer a variety of perspectives, from the effects of social conditions and social changes to conflicts within the individual, from difficulties relating to family, school, and career to the influence of genes and brain chemistry. In this viewpoint, we will examine explanations that have been offered from each of these perspectives. . . .

The Sociological Perspective

If the beginning of contemporary thinking about suicide can be identified with any one person, it would almost certainly be Émile Durkheim. . . . Considered one of the founding fathers of modern sociology, he was a pioneer in using statistical techniques to analyze social problems. Some of his most important ideas were originally published in an 1897 book titled *Le Suicide*. The ideas presented in this groundbreaking book about suicide remain influential to this day.

It is important to recognize that Durkheim theorized about suicide from a sociological perspective. He had little interest in looking for the reasons for suicide within the individual person; rather, he was interested in studying the suicide rates of groups and the society as a whole. . . .

Durkheim was able to show that suicide was somewhat higher among

> *"[Durkheim's] theory linked suicide to diminished social integration."*

unmarried people than married people and that communities in which the ratio of Catholics to Protestants was relatively high had lower rates of suicide. He used the provinces of Bavaria for this latter demonstration. These statistics were important, not so much in themselves, but because they supported an evolving theory. The theory linked suicide to diminished social integration. In Durkheim's view, a social unit that is cohesive will tend to have lower suicide rates among its members. Durkheim stated the hypothesis succinctly: "So we reach the general conclusion: suicide varies inversely with the degree of integration of the social groups of which the individual forms a part." Durkheim believed that the hypothesis was far-reaching, holding for domestic society (i.e., the family), religious society and political society. . . .

Durkheim's theories have given rise to research on suicide. Following Durkheim, we would expect that the fragmentation of a social unit in which the members had clear-cut responsibilities and interdependencies would promote suicidal reactions. One of the most obvious cases of such a social unit is the contemporary family. Studies of suicide rates of married people versus divorced people show precisely this pattern. For all age ranges considered—young adults (25 to 29) through senior citizens (65 to 69)—the suicide rates are higher for divorced people. Data reported in 1990 indicate that for the age range 25 to 29, the suicide rate for married males was 16 per 100,000 people, whereas the rate for divorced males was 70 per 100,000. Comparable figures for females were 5 per 100,000 for married women and 20 per 100,000 for divorced women. The suicide rates were four to five times higher for divorced people. These data support Durkheim's views, although they are also consistent with psychologically oriented explanations that emphasize the effects of loss.

Another area of research stimulated by Durkheim's writings is the relation of church membership and suicide rates. Durkheim proposed that religions that emphasized large numbers of shared beliefs, practices, and rituals would tend to foster low suicide rates. Following Durkheim, researchers have compared the suicide rates of Catholics and Protestants. Statistics collected as far back as the early years of the [twentieth] century indicated that the suicide rate of Catholics has tended to be lower. In recent years, however, researchers such as Steven

Stack have questioned the simple comparison of Catholics and Protestants, pointing out that there are wide differences among Protestant denominations. And indeed studies have reported considerable variation among Protestant groups in terms of suicide rates. Stack further pointed out that not all studies found differences between Catholics and Protestants in suicide rates. A recent study by Bolger and his colleagues found no difference between Catholic university students and students of other faiths in terms of suicidal ideation. The question of religious differences in suicidal behavior has not been fully settled.

If we phrase the question in a somewhat different manner—whether church membership correlates with suicide rates—the answer appears to be "yes." R. Stark and his colleagues reported that in large American cities church membership was related to lower suicide rates.

One of the most powerful ways of shaking a person out of the fabric of modern society is to take away his or her job. Durkheim anticipated that such economic and social dislocation would increase the propensity toward suicide. And once again researchers have reported data consistent with Durkheim's analysis. There is a statistical link between unemployment and suicide. However, one cannot assume from the data that there is a direct causal link between unemployment and suicide.

> *"One of the most powerful ways of shaking a person out of the fabric of modern society is to take away his or her job."*

These various analyses, taken one at a time, generally support Durkheim's view that diminished social integration is associated with suicidal behavior. David Lester has carried the analysis a step further by discarding the piecemeal approach. Instead, he developed a more general measure of social integration that included a number of social variables, such as the divorce rate, interstate migration, church attendance, and the crime rate. Lester computed a numerical value for this measure for the individual states in the United States and looked at how rates of adolescent suicide varied with the measure. He found for males, for the age range 15 to 24, a substantial relation between the level of social integration—within the United States—and suicide. As Durkheim predicted, the less social integration, the higher the suicide rate. The finding could not be extended to females because the lower numbers of female suicide made the analysis unreliable.

Psychological Explanations

In discussing psychological analyses of suicide we will begin with the ideas of Sigmund Freud. Gifted with a searching intellect, Freud was among the first persons in our modern era to make significant contributions to the study of human personality. . . .

Freud offers a number of ideas to take note of when considering suicidal behavior: (1) the suicidal person may feel considerable anger toward another (or others); (2) this anger may be turned inwardly against oneself, ultimately resulting in acts of self-destruction; and (3) people entertain these death wishes on an unconscious level; i.e., they are unaware of them.

Turning anger originally directed toward others inwardly in an unconscious process is an idea that Freud also mentions in another context—the genesis of depression. Suicide and depression are associated; depression is a characteristic emotional state of many persons attempting suicide. There is considerable evidence to support the view that people who direct their anger toward themselves tend to have higher levels of depression. For example, Roland Tanck and I carried out a study in which we asked college students to keep diaries for a period of ten days. In the diaries, we included questions asking whether the students had felt angry during the day. When they responded "yes," we asked them, "What was it that made you feel angry?" We found that the students who blamed themselves in these explanations were more likely to score higher on measures of depression. If feelings of anger are turned against oneself, is the risk of suicidal behavior increased? Freud's observations suggest that this is a pattern we should look for. . . .

Psychoanalytically oriented writers following Freud have expanded on his views, contributing new ideas to the study of suicide. Karl Menninger's book, *Man Against Himself,* is an important statement. Another writer, Herbert Hendin, made some interesting observations about young, disturbed, suicidal patients in psychiatric wards. Hendin noted strong feelings of guilt and the need for self-punishment among these young patients. He reported that they often felt worthless, deserving of punishment, and filled with self-hatred. Hendin viewed their suicide attempts as a kind of self-punishment for delusions of guilt and sin. . . .

Hendin wrote that suicidal acts or gestures can serve the motivation of forcing affection from unwilling people. The suicidal gesture communicates the idea, "Look what you are driving me to; you will have to treat me better." Viewed this way, a suicide attempt can serve the function of emotional blackmail. . . .

Psychologist Edwin Shneidman has worked on the problem of suicide for many years and has written extensively about it. In studying suicidal individuals, he has noted ten common features of suicide. His list provides a useful framework for thinking about the problem. These common features are:

> *"Depression is a characteristic emotional state of many persons attempting suicide."*

1) The purpose of the act is to seek a solution.
2) The goal is to end consciousness.
3) The stimulus is intolerable psychological pain.
4) The source of stress is frustrated psychological needs.
5) The emotion experienced is hopelessness/helplessness.

6) The cognitive state is ambivalence.

7) The perceptual state is constriction.

8) The action is escape.

9) The interpersonal action is communication of intention.

10) The consistency is lifelong patterns of coping.

Shneidman provides detailed descriptions of these ten common features of suicidal people. Here are a few examples. When he writes about the purpose of suicide, he points out that suicide is not a random, purposeless act. On the contrary, to the distressed person it seems to be the only answer to the problem. In describing pain, he speaks of it as psychological pain, using such terms as "intolerable" and "unendurable." This psychological pain is viewed as the "center of suicide" and is the chief hurdle that must be dealt with if life-saving efforts are to be successful. Shneidman's view is that if the level of pain can be lowered—even by a small amount—the individual can choose to live. In writing about "constriction," he sees it as a transient state in which the options one sees for oneself are narrowed. The person is in a state of mental blinders. He or she has tunnel vision, seeing a limited range of choices. Finally, in discussing the communication of intention, Shneidman points out that most suicide victims provide some kind of verbal or behavioral clues that signal the impending suicidal act. These clues may range from signals of distress to actually saying goodbye to people. . . .

> *"Most suicide victims provide some kind of verbal or behavioral clues that signal the impending suicidal act."*

Biological Explanations

When Denise was twelve, her father committed suicide. When Denise was eighteen, she was hospitalized for a suicide attempt following the breakup of a love affair. Her mother looked at her other children protectively and wondered, "Was it something in the family—was it something in the genes?"

Suicide, like some forms of mental illness, tends to run in families, occurring more often than one would expect by chance. In a paper reviewing this evidence, Alec Roy noted that in his own research almost half of 248 patients with a family history of suicide had attempted suicide themselves.

Now if it is true that one's risk of attempting suicide is greater if there has been a suicide in the family, does that necessarily imply that the connection is genetic? The answer, of course, is *no*. Alternative social learning explanations can be easily put forth. A child models the behavior of his or her parents; if a parent is depressed and suicidal, the child may pick up these tendencies in much the same way he or she picks up other behavior patterns from parents. The clustering of suicides within families, however, raises suspicions of genetic involvement, and other lines of evidence support the hypothesis that genetic influences play a role in suicide. . . .

Suicide

It has been recognized for some years that many people who are clinically depressed have low levels of the neurotransmitter serotonin, a chemical that is used in the transmission of signals in the brain. Because many people who attempt suicide are depressed, it is a reasonable question to ask whether serotonin levels play a role in suicide as well. Researchers have looked at the cerebrospinal fluid levels of the serotonin metabolite (5-HIAA) and reported that low cerebrospinal fluid 5-HIAA levels are associated with suicidal behavior in depressed patients and in some other clinical groups as well. The most clear-cut results have been found for individuals making violent suicide attempts that involve shooting or hanging.

In addition to studies of people attempting suicide, researchers have carried out postmortem examinations of the brains of people who have committed suicide. In his review article, Roy notes that some of these neurochemical analyses have found decreases in serotonin, or in its metabolite 5-HIAA, in the brain stems or frontal cortex. Although a linkage between serotonin and suicide has not been reported by all investigators, enough evidence has been compiled to indicate that this chemical may play a part in the suicidal process. . . .

All of these theories and ideas, whether sociological, psychological, or biological, are offered as explanations for suicidal behavior across the age span.

Homosexuality Is a Factor in Teen Suicide

by Chris Hamilton

About the author: *Chris Hamilton is a former staff reporter for the* Minnesota Daily.

University senior Erin Ferguson considers herself one of the lucky ones.

When she told her parents in junior high she was a lesbian, her family was supportive. When she entered St. Paul Central High School, there was a gay, lesbian, bisexual and transgender group that met after classes let out.

Her family and friends were railings on which she pulled herself up and away from the grasp of adolescent depression. She and many medical and counseling professionals claim stress brings on this form of depression. Being homosexual in the conformist and often homophobic atmosphere of junior and senior high schools drives many to make extreme choices.

"If friends, family and school are not supportive, it's hard to do well," said Ferguson. "When you have to be hiding who you are all the time, some kids I knew left home or dropped out instead. And some I knew were on that track, but they got in the support group and that changed."

A Sense of Despair

If untreated, the sense of despair kids feel when they don't flow with the mainstream can lead to suicide.

Although a recent University study said homosexuality and bisexuality are not significant factors in suicide attempts, suicidal thoughts or suicide intentions for teenage girls, the same cannot be said for the boys.

The study, published in an August edition of the *American Journal of Public Health*, claimed homosexual or bisexual junior high school and senior high school boys are seven times more likely than heterosexual boys of the same age to report suicide attempts.

The research said 131 male respondents identified themselves as "bisexual or mostly/100 percent homosexual." More than 28 percent of them reported sui-

Excerpted from "Researchers Study Sexual Orientation and Suicide," by Chris Hamilton, *The Minnesota Daily,* September 25, 1997. Reprinted with permission.

cide attempts. That is compared to more than 4 percent of heterosexual counterparts claiming suicide attempts.

Traditionally, females are up to nine times more likely to attempt suicide than males, according to American Association of Suicidology documents. Males, though, are six times more likely to complete a suicide, a fact attributed to greater handgun use for suicide by males.

The University findings placed heterosexual girls in the 14 percent range for reported suicide attempts. About 20 percent of homosexual or bisexual teenage girls responded similarly.

> *"Being homosexual in the conformist and often homophobic atmosphere of junior and senior high school drives many to make extreme choices."*

Researchers used the findings to suggest that homosexuality/bisexuality in itself is not a lone determiner of suicide risk for teens. Heterosexual and homosexual or bisexual girls had nearly uniform rates of suicidal thoughts or intent. These statistics led researchers to conclude that sexual orientation is not the cause of suicide attempts because it does not operate that way in girls.

Instead, researchers point to other factors for the high rates of reported suicide attempts for gay males. Factors such as verbal and physical harassment, substance use or isolation of boys thought of as sexually different than their heterosexual peers contribute to their high rates of suicide.

"In prior research, gender nonconformity has been found to be a risk factor for young gay males to attempt suicide," said Dr. Gary Remafedi, lead author of the study and an associate professor of pediatrics at the University. "It may have more serious consequences for boys than for girls. Boys thought to be effeminate are likely to be the subject of more maltreatment than girls who are tomboyish."

Remafedi said he hoped his research would help clinicians recognize that teens struggling with coming out are at risk. Terry Haugen-Sjostrom, the clinical director for the Crisis Connection, a nonprofit helpline, is not surprised by the study's findings. She also attributes the rates to the forced separation by their peers that many gay teen males encounter.

The Stress of a Homophobic Society

"The study certainly fits our anecdotal experience," said Haugen-Sjostrom. "They certainly feel isolated socially. Our values say that to be homosexual is to be different. In adolescence, finding out who we are, who we want to fall in love with, is our job. So to find you are someone not accepted by the culture makes it hard to go on."

Beth Zemsky, director of the University's Gay, Lesbian, Bisexual and Transgender Programs Office, said the study is consistent with previous research.

She also said our culture's intolerance of homosexuality, which can often be violent, leads many to take their own life.

"Suicide attempts are often caused by the stress of a homophobic society," said Zemsky. "The study is in line with the American Psychiatric Association. People are not killing themselves because they are gay, but because they are dealing with a society that discriminates."

Matt Strickler, 20, is a sophomore at the University. He told his family and friends he was gay when he was still in junior high in Rochester. Coming out would eventually provide him with the inner strength to deal with the discrimination he encountered at school.

"I still got called a faggot even before I came out," said Strickler. "But the more I came out the more confident I became, and I was targeted less. I became more sure of myself, so I was less likely to take the crap people gave me. I would do something about it.

"When I first came out I tended to be ashamed because I was different. I wouldn't tell or protest. When people are looking for a target, it's usually someone who's hiding or ashamed."

Strickler's self-confidence was bolstered even more after attending the Arts High School in Golden Valley, a place where students tended to be much more accepting of those who were gay. Although he did not sink to the depths of seriously considering suicide, he understands why others would.

"I did see it with other people," said Strickler. "Things got better only for me after I came out. That's what I had to do to survive, but I could definitely see how day in and day out taking that kind of abuse could lead someone to consider suicide."

Support Systems Are Necessary

Strickler attributed his success to the support systems around him. Without family, friends and a gay support group in his hometown, he said the isolation would have been insurmountable.

"There were times when I did feel completely alone with no one to talk to or understand my problems," said Strickler. "A lot of shame and despair comes from feeling like you're the only one. Finding other people was really key to my survival."

Nationally, teen suicide is growing at alarming rates. Since 1960, the number of teen suicides has tripled in the United States, according to the Centers for Disease Control and Prevention. Those under the age of 25

"Boys thought to be effeminate are likely to be the subject of more maltreatment than girls who are tomboyish."

accounted for 16 percent or nearly 5,000 suicides in 1992. These statistics have sent many in the health community searching for reasons behind the jump.

In 1989, the U.S. Department of Health and Human Services released a report stating that up to a third of all teen suicides were committed by gay youths. The validity of these findings has been at the heart of heated debate ever since.

The University study is one attempt to legitimize the relationship between homosexuality/bisexuality and suicide.

The study utilized data from a 1987 survey of more than 36,000 Minnesota students in grades seven to 12. The survey was filled out by 95 percent of the students. Researchers from the University's Youth and AIDS Project said their "unbiased" findings end contentions over whether there is a relationship between homosexuality and suicide.

"For many experts there has been a controversy about these issues because prior studies were done on volunteer samples," said Remafedi.

"I think this study is important because it resolves controversy about issues and provides very hard evidence of the link between suicide and homosexuality in males," Remafedi said.

A Need for Education and Communication

From there, many in the gay or health care communities would like to see solutions that involve opening up education and communication surrounding adolescent sexual orientation issues. This could involve school programs that deal frankly with homosexuality in an attempt to end the social stigma attached to it.

"The solutions are about changing the environment in school, so a boy can walk down a hall without fear of ostracism or violence," Zemsky said.

Ann DeGroot, executive director of the Gay and Lesbian Community Action Council, located in Minneapolis, is a proponent of school programs aimed at diffusing homophobia through knowledge and discussion. She said these programs would help ease suicidal tendencies in gay youths.

"Our culture's intolerance of homosexuality, which can often be violent, leads many to take their own life."

"I'd like to see more school-based programs," said DeGroot. "Staff and teachers need to learn not to allow homophobic behavior. High schoolers need access to good counselors and information. We need to open up the discussion and dialogue. This research shows the consequences of keeping this information repressed."

Remafedi said he hopes his study helps bring to light the problem of homophobia and its consequences.

"There's a message to society in it, to change the underlying conditions that lead young people to commit desperate acts."

Suicide Among Homosexual Teens Is Exaggerated

by Delia M. Rios

About the author: *Delia M. Rios is a writer for Newhouse News Service.*

At the end of an interview with actress Ellen DeGeneres, aired the night her lesbian television character "came out," anchor Diane Sawyer addressed viewers of "PrimeTime Live":

"And as we close, we're going to repeat a government statistic that a gay teen-ager is some three times as likely to attempt suicide as another teen-ager. Ellen DeGeneres has said whatever happens to her, tonight's broadcast was in part to hold on to them."

It's a statistic that's been repeated innumerable times.

The trouble is, there is no scientifically valid evidence that it's true.

That was the conclusion—back in 1994—of representatives of the Centers for Disease Control, the National Institute of Mental Health, the American Psychological Association, the American Association of Suicidology, and gay and lesbian advocacy and service groups, among others.

They had met to see if there was a link between gay teens and suicide, which had been propelled into public consciousness by a single essay included in a 1989 U.S. Department of Health and Human Services report on youth suicide.

Their finding was this:

"There is no population-based evidence that sexual orientation and suicidality are linked in some direct or indirect manner."

Joyce Hunter, the immediate past president of the National Lesbian and Gay Health Association, participated in that 1994 meeting.

"What we're saying is that we don't know," Hunter says.

Yet the stunningly high number of suicide attempts represented by the "two to three times more likely" figure—along with an unsubstantiated, companion

Reprinted from "No Scientific Evidence for Link Between Gay Teens, Suicide," by Delia M. Rios, *The San Diego Union-Tribune*, May 26, 1997. Reprinted by permission of New House News Service.

statistic that gays and lesbians may account for 30 percent of completed teen suicides—has shaped public perceptions of gay teens for nearly a decade.

They are portrayed as emotionally vulnerable and as victims of an oppressive larger culture who require society's intervention. But Hunter agrees with mental health researchers that most gay and lesbian teens, like teens overall, are emotionally resilient people who "go on to develop a positive sense of self and who go on with their lives."

> *"There is no . . . evidence that sexual orientation and suicidality are linked in some direct or indirect manner."*

Gay advocates and critics—as well as the national press from *The New York Times* to the *Chicago Tribune* to the *Los Angeles Times*—have cited the suicide link so often that it has become conventional wisdom with the power to influence public policy. Governor William F. Weld of Massachusetts, for instance, cited this suicide statistic as a driving force behind his state's creation of a Commission on Gay and Lesbian Youth.

Overall, some 5,000 adolescents commit suicide in the United States every year. No one is certain how many may be gay, lesbian or bisexual.

Peter Muehrer is chief of the Youth Mental Health program in the Prevention and Behavioral Medicine Research Branch of the National Institute of Mental Health. He has evaluated the major research studies that are most often cited to support a link between sexual orientation and suicide. He has concluded that the research is "limited in both quantity and quality."

Research Is Difficult

Muehrer noted the difficulties in quantifying suicides among gay teen-agers. Suicide research, in general, is difficult. There is no agreement on standard definitions, so that it is unclear even what constitutes a suicide "attempt." And there are no reliable or standard methods for measuring suicide attempts.

All of which is further complicated when looking at suicide and sexual orientation. Death certificates do not list whether an individual is heterosexual or homosexual. And, as Hunter points out, gays and lesbians—whether adults or teens—may not be inclined to identify themselves to researchers conducting general population studies.

For those reasons, according to Muehrer, ". . . it is not possible to accurately compare suicide attempt rates between gay and lesbian youth and non-gay youth in the general population."

So where did those shockingly high numbers come from?

The "two to three times more likely to attempt suicide" and "30 percent completed suicide" figures so often cited in discussions of gay teens and suicide originated in an article written by Paul Gibson, a licensed clinical social worker in San Francisco. He was among those asked to submit a report to the Task Force on Youth Suicide at the Department of Health and Human Services in

1989. Of the 50 papers included in the task force report, two—including Gibson's—addressed suicide and sexual orientation.

Gibson says his report was not a research study. It included no original field research. It was a review of existing research out of which he drew the "two to three times more likely" number. He used that figure to estimate that 30 percent of completed teen suicides are by gays and lesbians.

Muehrer, having reviewed major studies that Gibson cites, wrote that "there is no scientific evidence to support this (30 percent) figure."

"Only two relatively recent community-based original research studies have examined the sexual orientation of individuals who completed suicide," he wrote. "Both found that between 2.5 and 5 percent of the suicides in their overall samples were by people believed to be gay."

Times Have Changed

Among the research weaknesses Muehrer found in the other studies was that "several of the key published sources are based on interviews with gay and lesbian adults in the early 1970s, asking them to recount their adolescence years earlier.

"Even if problems of retrospective bias could be overcome, the pace of change in North American culture for lesbian, gay male, and bisexual youths has been so rapid that the adolescent experiences of current gay and lesbian adults may be of questionable validity with respect to the experiences of gay and lesbian adolescents in the 1990s."

Researchers have largely confined their work to "convenience samples"—that is, they've studied gay teens in runaway shelters and counseling centers. These are teens already in crisis and who may be more predisposed to suicide.

"Gay advocates and critics . . . have cited the suicide link so often that it has become conventional wisdom."

No one is discounting that some gay teens experience emotional distress or that some do attempt or commit suicide. Clinton W. Anderson of the American Psychological Association, who addresses gay, lesbian and bisexual issues and who was present at the 1994 workshop, says that the lack of "good science" on the issue should not be an excuse for not getting help to teens who need it. Clinicians who see teens in distress may not offer scientific evidence, Anderson argues, but neither should their observations be dismissed.

Depression Can Lead to Suicide

by Edward J. Dunne

About the author: *Edward J. Dunne is a division director at the American Association of Suicidology and a coauthor of* Suicide and Its Aftermath.

I recently interviewed a young woman whose father and brother had both completed suicide over 30 years ago. The woman was convinced that her father's suicide had been an act of spite directed towards his wife and children, particularly towards her older brother. Her father killed himself on Christmas day as family members were gathering in the home for dinner. He was in a special room he had fixed up in the garage ostensibly to be able to sleep during the day, but his daughter suspected that it was a way of keeping distance from his family. His relationship with her older brother had always been full of anger and invective. His suicide note mentioned everyone but the brother. Five years after her father ended his life, the older brother used the same gun to bring his life to an end.

As I listened to this story I recognized familiar themes: alcoholism and drug abuse, rages, parental demandingness, insensitivity, residual anger. When I questioned the woman more about her father, she painted a picture of a man who "could have had it all" but somehow failed to live up to his potential. He had been college educated with a very marketable specialty in engineering, yet somehow failed to keep early jobs which would have placed him on the right career track. Instead, when he ended his life he was working as a night watchman, a job his daughter felt he liked because of the isolation involved. The brother also had been an underachiever. After getting high marks in grade school and high school, and being offered a scholarship to college, he abruptly joined the Navy. His sister thought that this was his way of rebelling against his father—a sort of thumbing his nose at the family. But things did not go well in the Navy and he was soon discharged for alcoholism and using psychedelic drugs. Following this, he drifted for several years, going from hippie communes

Excerpted from "Depression . . . Depression . . . Depression!" by Edward J. Dunne, *Surviving Suicide,* vol. 10, no. 1, Spring 1998. Reprinted with permission from the author and the American Association of Suicidology.

to living on the road. He had been living at home for two months when he found the gun his father had used and put it to his own head.

Classic Signs of Depression

What was remarkable to me about this sad story was the woman's sense of guilt about her brother's death because she felt that she should have been able to undo the "damage" that her parent had inflicted on him and her complete acceptance of the early myth that her father's "meanness" was the root of the brother's suicide and the family misery. Even though she had been referred to me because of her own depression, she was not able to see the role depression played in her family's story. It had never occurred to her, nor to her surviving sister and mother, that her father evidenced classic signs of depression throughout most of his adult life. When, at my prompting, she asked her mother about her father's moods, she was surprised to discover that her mother thought of him as "dark" and "always unhappy," but had not thought that this was depression because he was not tearful, but attributed this moodiness to his failure to achieve. It simply hadn't occurred to any of them that the failure to achieve could have been a sign of depression. And, despite the fact that the father and son fought bitterly, she recalled that her mother and aunt had often remarked how alike they were in temperament.

> *"Our society generally downplays depression as a causative factor in suicide."*

Our society generally downplays depression as a causative factor in suicide. We say that a person killed himself because he was "despondent over a broken up love affair" or because he "got a low grade on a test" or because "she didn't get into the college of her choice." But such statements generally overlook the fact that many, many people have similar disappointments without ending their own lives. The difference is depression. Depression saps us of the ability to recover from adverse experiences. Depression, with its sense of hopelessness and helplessness, makes all failures or missed opportunities monumental in scope. These experiences feed on themselves—they produce even greater depression. But, because they like to view themselves as in control of their lives, depressed people rarely attribute these failures to anything other than their own flawed characters. Unfortunately, neither do those around them.

Genetic Factors Contribute to Suicide

by Shari Roan

About the author: *Shari Roan is a health writer for the* Los Angeles Times.

The sad chain of suicides that has plagued the talented Hemingway family for three generations may be due to a genetic trait passed unwittingly through the clan, say mental health experts.

The Los Angeles County coroner's office ruled Margaux Hemingway's July 1, 1996, death a suicide by massive barbiturate overdose. The former model's suicide is the fifth among four generations of relatives. Her famous grandfather, Ernest Hemingway, killed himself with a shotgun 35 years ago. The novelist's father, brother and sister also committed suicide.

But two or more suicides are not unusual in a family with a history. One in every four people who attempt suicide has a family member who also tried to commit suicide, according to a study of 2,304 Los Angeles residents completed several years ago by the National Institute of Mental Health.

"If you look at [the] spectrum of suicide behavior—attempts and completions—the majority of completers have a family history. It's the rule, not the exception, to have a history of suicidal behavior," says Dr. David Brent, a psychiatrist at the Western Psychiatric Institute in Pittsburgh and one of the nation's leading researchers on suicide.

Suicide is the eighth leading cause of death in the United States. Nearly 1% of Americans die by their own hand.

In most cases, people who succumb to suicide have an existing mental illness; usually depression or bipolar disorder, an illness that features bouts of depression alternating with manic behavior, Brent says. Some suicide victims are also substance abusers.

Inherited Traits

But studies even indicate there may be a specific gene or genes that increase the risk of suicide in certain families.

Reprinted from "Is There a Gene Behind Suicide?" by Shari Roan, *Los Angeles Times,* August 22, 1996. Reprinted by permission of the *Los Angeles Times.*

Studies have followed twins who were separated at birth or adopted children to tease apart the possible inherited tendencies toward suicide from environmental influences.

"A number of these studies suggest that suicide is associated with a family history but doesn't seem to be explained by psychiatric disorders alone," he says. "There is something else that is familially transmitted."

One researcher investigated an Amish community with high rates of depressive disorders. The study showed that suicides were clustered in particular families, with 73% of the suicides occurring in 16% of the families in the community, Brent says.

"There were two large pedigrees, both of whom were loaded with depressive illness, but only one pedigree was filled with suicide," Brent says.

What is it about this Amish family—and others—that leads its members to opt for suicide?

Despite this well-recognized pattern of family suicides, the answer still isn't clear, Brent says. But the question has ignited a number of research efforts to identify possible mechanisms in the brain that predispose people to suicide.

> *"There may be a specific gene or genes that increase the risk of suicide in certain families."*

One line of research has discovered low levels of a metabolite of serotonin—called 5-hydroxyindoleacetic acid—in the brains of people who commit suicide, a characteristic that may be inherited. Serotonin is a neurotransmitter that is involved in the control of impulses, particularly those involving aggression or violence.

People with this deficiency may be 10 times at greater risk of committing suicide, according to the 1995 book *Caring For the Mind* (Bantam), by Dianne Hales and Dr. Robert E. Hales.

"It's all a little shaky," says Brent of the research. "But many studies have been able to identify that these people are very low in something related to serotonin. This is the strongest single finding in this type of research."

Other studies also show these families have a tendency toward aggressive behavior.

"It seems aggression and family suicide is kind of interrelated," Brent says.

The weight of this evidence is so powerful that it weakens the theory that relatives of suicide victims tend to imitate the behavior.

"A Viable Option"

Part of the resounding impact of suicide on families is that relatives fear it runs in the family. Young people, in particular, worry that they will feel an irresistible urge to take their own lives, experts say.

When Joan Rivers' husband, Edgar Rosenberg, took his life several years ago, she said for other members of the family suicide then becomes "a viable option."

"After it becomes a reality in your family, it's a definite way out," Rivers was quoted as saying.

But studies show that imitation probably has limited influence, Brent says.

"We have done studies that look at the rate of suicidal behavior in families after a suicide, and we find very little imitation," he says. "I think imitation does take place. But our study suggests that the mechanism [for additional suicides] is other than imitation."

That concept offers little comfort to families with a history of suicide, Brent admits. Members wonder if they will feel powerless to control the urge to end their lives in moments of despair.

Survivors at Risk

"A lot of times survivors will ask me, 'Am I at increased risk?' The answer is that survivors are at fourfold increased risk. But I tell these people that suicide is still relatively rare. It's still unlikely they will kill themselves. On the other hand, they have the opportunity to be increasingly vigilant about the precursors."

The impact of suicide is usually greatest on the victim's offspring, says Heidi H. Spencer, a Bethesda, Md., psychotherapist and author of *Did I Do Something Wrong?* a book about the effects of mental illness on a family.

"It's especially significant for the offspring because the child or young adult identifies with a parent. They somehow experience that as one way of managing life's pain."

> *"Research has discovered low levels of a metabolite of serotonin . . . in the brains of people who commit suicide."*

The grief associated with a loved one's suicide may also kindle a desire for suicide.

"There is a yearning to be with that loved parent. The grieving is so hard to resolve that there is often an unconscious fantasy to reconnect with that parent."

There are other, less potent, factors that impinge on the moment when a suicide occurs. These include an easy means to kill—guns, a stockpile of drugs—and the absence of other people to thwart the act.

In Hemingway's case, those little extras may have allowed her to act on an inherited sensitivity. She had the drugs. And she was alone. She even fit the profile.

According to the Hales, unmarried women with a family history of suicide are more likely to attempt suicide than men or married women with similar backgrounds.

Chapter 3

Should Physicians Help Terminally Ill Patients Commit Suicide?

Chapter Preface

Two authors of viewpoints in the following chapter, Ben Mattlin and Geov Parrish, have severe disabilities. Both men are familiar with America's health care system, both have experienced extreme physical pain, and both are frustrated with the political powerlessness of the disabled. However, they hold opposing views on assisted suicide. For Parrish, the only person qualified to decide if a person's life is worth living is that person. Once an individual's life has become unendurable, he claims, the individual should be able to seek a painless end to suffering in assisted suicide, and neither the government nor anyone else should be able to interfere.

Mattlin, on the other hand, believes physicians should never be permitted to aid in the deaths of their patients. Permitting physicians to assist with suicides, he contends, could easily lead down a slippery slope to voluntary euthanasia—which involves a person's asking another to end his or her life—or even involuntary euthanasia—euthanasia that is not requested by the person receiving it.

Both Parrish and Mattlin seek to keep others from having control over their lives—the government in Parrish's case and physicians in Mattlin's. Most of the viewpoints in this chapter that oppose assisted suicide raise the slippery-slope issue, and most of those who advocate assisted suicide promote individual rights.

Physician-Assisted Suicide Is a Personal Choice

by **Geov Parrish**

About the author: *Geov Parrish is an active member of the War Resisters League.*

My perspective on this issue comes not only from my activism and pacifism, but also from the fact that I've survived multiple suicide attempts (the first when I was nine) and a terminal illness first diagnosed six years ago, for which I received an experimental multiple organ transplant two years ago.

As such, I'm probably above average in my appreciation of pain, depression and the pitfalls of medicine. And with those imperfections, I still believe absolutely that the only person qualified to make a decision about whether, with all available information, a life is or is not worth continuing, is the individual living that life. Nobody else: not a doctor, not a friend or family member, and especially not a government.

An Individual's Decision

I spent several years in degenerating physical condition. Though I was surrounded by caring, loving people, I knew each day that I was ultimately alone: Nobody else, no matter how well intentioned, understood or could understand my situation, what life was like waking each day in a body at war with itself. For someone whose situation is so acute that they cannot carry out suicide themselves, but require assistance, that isolation is likely to be even more powerful, and the concerns of the best-intentioned moralists and lobbyists even less relevant. They don't have to live in your body; you do.

Would assisted suicide save money for HMOs and other greedy health care providers? Probably. Should we keep agonized individuals alive to spite those HMOs? No. Can friends, family members, or doctors exert powerful, selfish influences over an individual's decision? Of course. Yet this happens in every medical decision. We don't deny a woman the right to abortion because she

Reprinted from "A Simple, Basic Right," by Geov Parrish, *Nonviolent Activist.* Reprinted with permission. Article available at www.nonviolence.org/wrl/nva397-2.htm.

might be pressured into a bad decision; we defend her control over her body, and trust her judgment on what is invariably a wrenching decision.

Will some people make decisions that seem, in retrospect, tragic and impulsive? Probably. But how can you tell? . . .

To suggest that a terminally ill person is any less capable of independent judgment, when that person is far more likely to be in a situation none of the people around her or him have experienced, is insulting. Given that the people affected by assisted suicide laws are only those physically unable to act on their desire to die, it is also ablist and discriminatory. It is also cruel, selfish, and colonial. It is demanding that somebody stay alive, usually in misery, so as to conform to ethical standards of people whose lives don't remotely resemble theirs.

> *"The only person qualified to make a decision about whether . . . a life is . . . worth continuing, is the individual living that life."*

I am a pacifist because I believe in the sanctity of life. I also believe that life is an organic process, and death is a natural part of it. To be able to die, with dignity, in a manner of one's choosing, is both a sacred act and a simple and basic right. We have no business taking that right away.

Assisted Suicide Is a Fundamental Right

by Thomas A. Bowden

About the author: *Thomas A. Bowden is an attorney in private practice in Baltimore, Maryland. He is a member of the board of directors of the Association for Objective Law and a senior writer for the Ayn Rand Institute.*

On August 20, 1961, a Nobel Prize–winning physicist shot himself dead, leaving behind a suicide note whose poignant message reminds us of a truth that our society, thirty-five years later, still has not squarely faced.

Dr. Percy Bridgman, who was 79 years old, had been suffering through the final stages of terminal cancer. Wracked with pain and bereft of hope, he sought a way to end his life with dignity. But then, as now, it was illegal for a doctor to administer drugs intended to hasten death.

So Dr. Bridgman got a gun, and somehow he found the courage to pull the trigger, conscious of the fact that he was condemning others to the agony of discovering his bloody remains. As a final protest, he left a note that said simply: "It is not decent for society to make a man do this to himself. Probably this is the last day I will be able to do it myself."

The Supreme Court is presently considering whether states may make it a crime for doctors to assist in a patient's suicide. [The Supreme Court decided on June 26, 1997, that the U.S. Constitution does not prohibit states from banning physician-assisted suicide. The issue was thereby returned to the states. The Court acknowledged that its decision permitted the debate over assisted suicide to continue.] The issue is whether such laws violate the Constitutional rights of people like Dr. Percy Bridgman. In deciding these appeals, the Supreme Court must first resolve the threshold question: Whose life is it, anyway? Does your life belong to God, as the conservatives say? Or to society, as the liberals say? Or to you alone, as the Founding Fathers said?

The Declaration of Independence proclaimed, for the first time in the history of nations, that each person exists as an end in himself. This basic truth—which

Reprinted from "Assisted Suicide: A Moral Right," by Thomas A. Bowden. Reprinted with permission from the author and the Center for the Advancement of Objectivism. Article available at www.aynrand. org/medialink/suicide.html.

finds political expression in the right to life, liberty, and the pursuit of happiness—means in practical terms that you need no one's permission to live and that no one may forcibly obstruct your efforts to achieve your own personal happiness.

But what if happiness becomes impossible to attain? What if a dread disease, or some other calamity, drains all joy from life, leaving only misery and suffering? The right to life includes and implies the right to commit suicide. To hold otherwise—to declare that society must give you permission to kill yourself—is to contradict the right to life at its root. If you have a *duty* to live, despite your better judgment, then your life does not belong to you; you live by permission, not by right.

For these reasons, Dr. Bridgman had every right to decide the hour of his death and to implement that solemn decision as best he could. The choice was his because the *life* was his. And if a doctor had been willing to assist in the suicide, based on an objective assessment of his patient's mental and physical state, the law should not have stood in his way.

Religious conservatives, by contrast, reject the whole idea of individual rights, asserting that your life is a gift from God and that you are put on earth to fulfill a divine plan. Not surprisingly, therefore, conservatives shrink in revulsion from the very idea of suicide. According to them, one who decides to "play God" by causing his own death, or assisting in the death of another, insults his Maker and invites eternal damnation.

The Supreme Court's conservative bloc would never explicitly adopt such reasoning, because the First Amendment forbids the establishment of religion. But there are other ways of enacting religious dogma into law, as proven by the 1986 case of *Bowers v. Hardwick*. In that case, the Supreme Court approved laws that criminalize consensual sodomy. Untroubled by the lack of a secular basis for such laws, the Court ruled, in effect, that citizens in a democracy may vote away individual rights, even if that vote is based ultimately on nothing but religious faith.

> *"Whose life is it, anyway? . . .*
> *Does your life belong to*
> *God, . . . to society, . . .*
> *or to you alone?"*

Unfortunately, the liberals' alternative is no better. Your life, they say, belongs not to God but to society. Thus, if you should conclude that life holds no joy and it is time to die with dignity, a court must "weigh" your desire against the supposed interests of society. If the resulting "balance" tips in favor of society's demands, then you must go on suffering—and your doctor must watch helplessly—until the last bitter paroxysm carries you to the grave.

The conservatives appear poised for victory in the current appeals. But even if the Supreme Court were to approve the practice of assisted suicide, based on some arbitrary "balancing" act, the ruling would not be a victory for the individual's inviolable right to life. Instead, it would simply announce that society, for the time being, and only until further notice, has decided to grant you and your doctor, in certain limited circumstances, *permission* to end your life.

Legislators alone cannot destroy this country—they need assistance from judges who are willing to look the other way as individual rights are violated. The Supreme Court's abject willingness to render such assistance, in thousands of cases involving vital liberties, has placed America's very survival in doubt. The irony here is that by helping lawmakers kill the basic political principle on which our survival depends—the principle of individual rights—the Supreme Court has become the nation's most dangerous practitioner of assisted suicide.

Religious Groups Should Not Dictate How People Should Die

by Faye Girsh

About the author: *Faye Girsh is the executive director of the Hemlock Society USA. This viewpoint is the text of a speech presented by Girsh before the American Atheists' St. Louis conference on January 26, 1999.*

Since 1980, the Hemlock Society has argued that physician-assisted dying should be one option in the continuum of care at the end of life. Most people in this country agree. Polls repeatedly show that at least two thirds of the population support this choice, including a majority of Catholics. And not only is the sentiment in this country supportive of assisted dying, but more than 70% of the population in Canada, Australia, the United Kingdom, and in Europe want this option. Where the population is predominantly Catholic—such as in Quebec, Spain, and France—the support is even higher. In Colombia, a Catholic country, the equivalent of our Supreme Court declared in 1997 that physician aid in dying is not a crime.

Minority Rule

If there is so much support for the idea, why isn't it happening? Let's examine what just occurred in Michigan on November 3rd, 1998. Seventy-one percent of the voters said *No* to Proposal B, which would have legalized assistance in dying by a doctor under strict safeguards. The repeated, deceptive advertisements broadcast on TV six weeks before the election, at a cost of more than five million dollars, worked to dissuade the 70% of the voters who were initially favorable to physician assisted dying.

A front organization was set up calling itself Citizens for Compassionate Care; 90% of the money for their anti-campaign came from Catholic sources. Here are some of the large donations: $250,000 was donated from the US Catholic Confer-

Reprinted from "The Pope Wants to Tell You How to Die: Will You Stand for It?" by Faye Girsh, *American Atheist,* Spring 1999. Reprinted with permission from the American Atheist Press.

ence, an amazing $1,080,000 from the Archdiocese of Detroit, another $1,750,000 from other dioceses in Michigan, $50,000 from the Catholic Health Association, and a mere $125,000 from the Daughters of Charity. Michigan Right to Life, which has worked with the Catholic Church to undermine this initiative, contributed $135,000. Cardinal Maida, in Detroit, made nine-minute video tapes against physician aid in dying. Thousands of copies were distributed all over the state together with letters decrying suicide as a sin. On the Sunday before the election he even spoke to the two largest *Baptist* congregations in Detroit!

Merian's Friends, the sponsors of the assisted dying proposal, spent $900,000 just to get the signatures to qualify it for the ballot and had $75,000 left to run the campaign. They were outspent $5.5 million to $75,000, or a 74:1 ratio. The Hemlock Society USA, through our political arm PRO-USA, contributed $75,000—money from the grass-roots supporters to gather signatures and then to run the actual campaign. That's a lot of money for Hemlock, but nothing compared to the corporate contributions by the Catholic Church and its tax-free "charitable" organizations. Doesn't this raise a question about the inordinate influence of one religious group over the most intimate practices—how they die—of people who have no interest or belief in that religion?

The Power of the Church

An interesting poll taken after this election showed that the No vote on Proposal B was correlated with church attendance. Only 13% of people who attended church services weekly voted to legalize physician aid in dying compared with 51% of people who said they attended church "almost never." Differences between church attendees and non-attendees is significant and profound and probably extends into many areas of belief.

In November, 1994, Oregonians voted to legalize physician aid in dying. After extraordinary lobbying, the legislature tried to reverse the will of the people and sent an initiative to rescind their vote back to them in November, 1997. More than $4 million dollars was spent to rescind that vote, mostly from Catholic sources. Fortunately, the opposition was not able to get away with their religious domination. Not coincidentally, Oregon has the least number of people with a religious affiliation of any state. When Catholic leaders and the religious right saw this happening, they geared up to make sure it would not happen in Michigan. In two years the people of Maine will vote on this and, again, the Catholic Church, with the Right to Life groups, are preparing to get millions of dollars in contributions from Catholic organizations (to say nothing of large Catholic individual donors).

> *"The sponsors of the assisted dying proposal . . . were outspent . . . [by] a 74:1 ratio [by the Catholic Church]."*

In Congress, leaders of the religious right introduced a bill to punish doctors who prescribed medications to help terminally ill, suffering patients die. The Hyde-Nickles bill was withdrawn during the last session in the house and senate, primarily because of opposition from the American Medical Association (AMA) and forty other medical, nursing, and pain groups. They argued that the bill would have restricted the prescribing of adequate pain medication. Both sponsors have sworn to reintroduce it in some form. This is how Henry Hyde thinks about this issue:

> We must protect life, the intrinsic value of human life, no matter how wretched. . . . It is stated in our constitution that we have an inalienable right to life. I believe we have that inalienable right from the time of conception to natural death.

This philosophy means that every fertilized egg has to become a child—despite the wishes of the woman carrying it—and every life must end "naturally" despite the suffering of that patient, the medical technology which is extending that life, the loss of any quality in that life, and the insistent wish of that person to end the suffering by death.

The Church Exercises Its Power

The wish to extend life for life's sake can be respected. It is the case, however, that many doctors and hospitals will not provide medical care which is considered futile. Preserving biological existence regardless of its quality—and regardless of the wishes of the person whose existence it is—is immoral and, in many cases, amounts to the torture of the patient and his or her family. The question at issue is whether certain people have a right to impose their values on others who do not hold those values. We cannot permit people to essentially be tortured, to lose their dignity, to endure the distortion of their life story because some religious groups feel that only God can take a life or that suicide is a mortal sin. These are beliefs which have no empirical base, which are a matter of faith, and with which many if not most Americans disagree. Justice Steven Reinhardt wrote for the majority in the 1996 9th Circuit decision in *Washington v Glucksberg:*

> *"In Congress, leaders of the religious right introduced a bill to punish doctors who prescribed medications to help terminally ill, suffering patients die."*

> Those who believe strongly that death must come without physician assistance are free to follow that creed, be they doctors or patients. They are not free, however, to force their views, their religious convictions, or their philosophies on all the other members of a democratic society, and to compel those whose values differ with theirs to die painful, protracted, and agonizing deaths.

Many Hemlock members have a strong belief in God but see their deity as merciful and one who has given us choice and intellect to be able to make these decisions. For those who are not theists it is insulting to thrust this value on them and insist that they die a certain way to please someone else's god. As legal scholar and philosopher Ronald Dworkin said,

> Making someone die in a way others approve, but he believes a horrifying contradiction of his life, is a devastating, odious form of tyranny.

Turning Back the Clock

The religious right is not only opposed to physician aid in dying, they want to turn the clock back so that the decision in the case of Nancy Cruzan (1990) by the US Supreme Court would be in danger. In that case the Court upheld the right of all Americans to refuse unwanted medical treatment, including food and water, and to designate proxies to make their health-care decisions for them if they were unable. The Hugh Finn case in Virginia was an example of where these sentiments lie and how even the Governor could be illegally influenced to intervene in a situation in which he had no legal right.

> *"Preserving biological existence regardless of its quality . . . is immoral and, in many cases, amounts to the torture of the patient."*

Mr. Finn was a TV announcer who, in 1995, was in a severe car accident which left him in a persistent vegetative state. [In 1999] his wife asked that he be removed from artificial food and hydration and allowed to die. Religious relatives got into the act, contacted Virginia Right to Life, which picketed, held press conferences, and cast aspersions on his wife because she said Finn would never have wanted to live that way. They enlisted the Republican governor who decreed that Finn's life support could not be removed. Fortunately, the Supreme Court of Virginia made it clear that the law was on his wife's side and Mr. Finn was allowed to die (albeit by removal of the feeding tubes, thus by dehydration).

How important is it to our lives to have the right to die? Let me quote from Dr. Charles McKhann, a professor of surgery at Yale, a member of the Hemlock Medical Advisory Board and author of the recent book, *A Time to Die: A Place for Physician Assistance:*

> The cruel fact is that death comes to some only after such prolonged disability and intolerable pain that the person feels emotionally naked and deprived of any real humanity. A dignified life deserves a dignified death. . . . It seems beyond reason that people who manage their affairs successfully in life should turn over the management of their death and dying to others. . . . Some observers fear that allowing physicians to assist in dying would desensitize them to the value of life.

> My own experience, and that of all physicians with whom I have spoken, is just the opposite. The value of life assumes a new dimension when you have personally helped to bring it to an end.

The government should not interfere with the right to control the time and manner of our dying with medical assistance. Some, like Dr. Kevorkian, believe it should be governed only by the medical boards of each state, as are nearly all medical procedures. He is a physician who has sacrificed his license, and now may face the loss of his liberty and even his life for this principle. [In 1998] the Supreme Court overturned two appellate court decisions which agreed that state prohibitions against physician assistance in dying violated the 14th Amendment. Unfortunately, the Supreme Court disagreed that it was a constitutional right and left the matter for the states to decide. As democratic as that appears, it ignores the fact that legislators are strongly influenced by pressure groups such as the Catholic Church, and that statewide initiatives are often won by the side with the most money.

Oregon's Right-to-Die Legislation

It has also been argued that the state should have minimal control over our lives; this would be accomplished by allowing the practice of physician assistance to be decriminalized without any specific provisions. Decriminalization has never been seriously considered in any state legislature. Since 1988, the Hemlock Society, with other right-to-die organizations, have proposed state ballot initiatives which would permit the practice, but under careful safeguards. This is the kind of law that was passed by the people of Oregon. Here are the provisions of that law:

• A competent, terminally ill adult must make repeated requests over a period of time.

• Two doctors must confirm the terminal diagnosis.

• A psychological examination is an option if the physicians are concerned about depression, incompetence, or coercion.

• An oral request must be confirmed in writing and reiterated orally after a waiting period.

• All alternatives must be explained to the patient.

• If the patient still wants a hastened death, a prescription for lethal medication is written.

• The patient may choose to take the medication when his/her suffering is too great.

> *"The question at issue is whether certain people have a right to impose their values on others who do not hold those values."*

• Neither loved ones nor a physician in attendance is subject to criminal or civil penalties.

• The doctor reports the death to the state health department keeping the name of the patient confidential.

Although this may sound bureaucratic and complex, it dramatically reduces state interference in the very personal process of dying. This law provides the kinds of safeguards which ensure that people who could continue their lives do so. The Oregon Death with Dignity Act has been in effect since November, 1997, and has been used by a small number of dying patients whose death was peaceful, quick, and gentle. Some-one said this about it:

> This is a permissive law. It allows something. It requires nothing. It forbids nothing and taxes no one. It enhances freedom. It lets people do a little more of what they want, without hurting anyone else. It removes a slight bit of the weight of government regulation that hangs over all of us all the time if we step out of line. So why are the opponents so dead set on getting the law overturned?

The Hemlock Society provides information and counseling to people who are contemplating a hastened death or are generally planning for a peaceful death and want to know all the options available to them. Until assisted dying is legal in the 49 other states, we will continue to supply information about self-deliverance, advance directives, hospice care, nursing homes, pain management, and other options. Suicide is never a solution for temporary distress. Suicide shortens the living process; we argue for an option to shorten the dying process.

"For those who are not theists it is insulting to . . . insist that they die a certain way to please someone else's god."

Hemlock does believe that, as a part of the continuum of care available at the end of life, assisted dying with medical help should be an option. We support hospice and better pain relief but even with the best end of life care, a small number of people will choose to hasten their dying process and this should be available so that people can choose a gentle, peaceful, quick and certain death in the company of their loved ones. Knowing that there is a way out will actually extend life.

Physician-Assisted Suicide Is an Ethical Response to Extreme Suffering

by Timothy Quill, interviewed by Tom Duffy

About the authors: *Timothy Quill is a physician and professor at the University of Rochester School of Medicine and Dentistry. He is a leading proponent of the assisted-suicide movement. Tom Duffy is a correspondent and frequent contributor to* People Weekly.

For many Americans, Dr. Jack Kevorkian is the celebrity centerpiece of the furious debate over assisted suicide. But a case being considered by the U.S. Supreme Court could have far more impact on how doctors handle terminally ill patients who want to die. Deeply involved in it is Dr. Timothy E. Quill, a respected internist and a professor at the University of Rochester School of Medicine and Dentistry. Quill, 47, risked a 15-year jail term in 1991 when he described in *The New England Journal of Medicine* how he had helped "Diane," a terminally ill cancer patient, hoard the barbiturates that eventually enabled her to take her own life. Though a Rochester, N.Y., grand jury refused to indict him, Quill was a lead plaintiff in a case challenging New York's assisted suicide ban. . . . [Quill won this case, but the decision was later overturned by the Supreme Court.]

Sharply critical of Kevorkian's methods, Quill—who is married to a former hospice nurse and has daughters, Carrie and Megan—is a reluctant activist who believes physician-assisted suicide should be carried out only as a last resort by doctors who have long-standing relationships with their patients. The author of the book *A Midwife Through the Dying Process,* he spoke with correspondent Tom Duffy.

Since assisted suicide has been practiced by doctors for decades, why didn't you just keep quiet about it?

The prevailing view was that while stopping life supports is ethically permissible, assisted suicide never is; one is perceived to be letting nature take its course, and one is perceived to be killing. We needed a serious discussion about this issue. I'd had this experience with Diane, and I decided that it was compelling. To me it wasn't a story about suicide but about working with individuals at the end of their life and about trying to give them as much choice as possible and where that takes you.

Could you describe a situation in which you believe helping a patient end a terminal illness would be the correct thing to do?

Robb, a patient with advanced AIDS, was hospitalized for an opportunistic infection. He suddenly took a turn for the worse and wasn't getting enough oxygen. As we were preparing to put him on a breathing machine, he said he didn't want to go on it; he was ready to call it quits.

We had his family in and challenged him to continue treatment. We tried to find alternatives that would allow him to keep going, but he wanted to stop. Ordinarily we like to make these decisions over a lot of time, but he was going rapidly downhill and so, after a long conversation, we let him choose not to go on the machine. He died over the next 12 hours. The family was able to say goodbye, and Robb was able to avoid a lingering death.

How is this different from patients Dr. Kevorkian has assisted?

Everything I do has to do with commitment to people over the long haul and careful assessment and making sure this is the last resort and that every patient has good access to hospice care and palliative care—the kinds of things that just don't exist for Kevorkian. He has frequently acted without knowing people in even the most superficial way. He has no experience in end-of-life care. He has no experience with people who are choosing to keep living. He's a pathologist, so he doesn't have the skills in pain management and psychological assessment. And he has his own agenda: He is fascinated with the moment of death and the machines of death.

What would you say to a doctor who maintains that his principal objective is to preserve life?

> *"[Kevorkian] has frequently acted without knowing people in even the most superficial way."*

The Hippocratic oath really has two dimensions. One is to preserve life and the other is to relieve human suffering. Usually you are trying to do both. But in end-of-life care you take relief of suffering as your priority, and you may use methods that may indirectly shorten life. People have a sense of who they are and what's important in life and want to die with that intact.

Are you concerned that legal assisted suicide could be abused by someone who didn't want the burden of caring for a gravely ill person?

People make these life-and-death decisions in secret right now. And if you want to see abuse, have a secret process that nobody is looking at.

What's paradoxical here is that we allow that kind of decision-making when it regards life-sustaining therapy, which patients have a right to choose not to accept. Once you make sure they are fully informed and are acting autonomously, they really have that right. To some degree the question of assisted suicide addresses that same issue: Do people at the end of their lives have to undergo more suffering than they feel they can endure? Who is to say they do, particularly since we have used medical technology to keep them alive longer and longer?

Do you ever regret having taken such a public stance?

I believe what I've done has promoted a discussion of what happens at the end of life, and that sustains me. The other thing that sustains me is that I think about the hassles I've gone through, and I compare them to those of my dying patients. Mine are small compared to theirs.

The Right to Die May Endanger the Disabled

by Ben Mattlin

About the author: *Ben Mattlin is a writer and editor in West Los Angeles.*

If I, a 33-year-old married Harvard graduate with a new baby daughter, threatened to hurl myself off a tall building, would an emergency medical team respond? And if one did, would I be offered counseling—or carbon monoxide?

Kevorkian's Methods Threaten the Disabled

I was born with a neuromuscular disability and use a wheelchair. With all the recent euthanasia news—Dr. Jack Kevorkian's acquittal and new trial and two federal court decisions favoring assisted suicide—I don't feel safe.

It may be constitutionally protected, but the right to die seems dangerous to those of us who are not ideal physical specimens.

I am not terminally ill. Both the April 2 [1996] decision by the Second U.S. Circuit Court of Appeals in New York and the March 6 decision by the Ninth U.S. Circuit Court of Appeals in San Francisco permit assisted suicide only for "a competent, terminally ill adult." But Judge Stephen Reinhardt, writing for the majority in San Francisco, went on to say that death is more humane than continuing to live in "a childlike state of helplessness."

They are not the same thing, though, this "state of helplessness" and being terminally ill. I have lived my whole life in such a state, needing assistance for eating, bathing, using the toilet. The humane thing to do is to help, not presume that my life isn't worth living.

Kevorkian isn't concerned with whether his clients' conditions are terminal. On Aug. 4, 1993, for example, after his medical license had been revoked in Michigan and California and Michigan's law against assisted suicide was in effect, Kevorkian aided the suicide of a 30-year-old who had recently become quadriplegic. Thomas Hyde wasn't terminally ill, not really ill at all. Nor was he in pain. His condition was roughly the same as mine.

In the new trial, Kevorkian stands accused in the death of Marjorie Wantz, 58,

Reprinted from "Walk a Mile in My Wheelchair," by Ben Mattlin, *Los Angeles Times,* April 12, 1996. Reprinted with permission from the author.

who, Kevorkian admits, was not terminally ill. Rather, Wantz "claimed after a series of surgeries to be suffering intense vaginal pain that they [prosecutors] contend was psychosomatic," the *New York Times* reported.

Granted, the people seeking assisted suicide want to die. And I believe in autonomy and self-determination; I am pro-choice. But what happens when able-bodied people attempt suicide? Why is their choice considered irrational? Why is a disabled person's suicide choice more readily judged sane?

Judging Quality of Life

Kevorkian would argue that he is ending suffering for people with no options. Tell that to Stephen Hawking, the physicist who has advanced amyotrophic lateral sclerosis, writes best-selling books, travels around the world and recently divorced his wife to marry his nurse. To say someone has no options just because doctors are stumped is medical arrogance. Quality of life is determined by more than physical condition.

To be sure, not everyone can be a Stephen Hawking. Which is precisely why Kevorkianism is so frightening. Does Kevorkian realize how hard it is for the average disabled person to feel valued in this society?

What I'm calling for is clarity. The right to die is appropriate only if it isn't clouded by fear and ignorance of disabilities. The dangers are potentially enormous. Euthanasia, after all, was one step toward the Holocaust. If doctors, judges and juries continue to cast doubts on the worth of people with disabilities, I fear for the one in six Americans (according to the census) who has a disability. If Kevorkian is truly concerned about us, why doesn't he join the cause of disability rights?

> *"Kevorkian isn't concerned with whether his clients' conditions are terminal."*

The U.S. Constitution Does Not Contain a Right to Assisted Suicide

by David R. Carlin Jr.

About the author: *David R. Carlin Jr. is a reporter for* Commonweal, *a magazine edited by Catholic laypeople.*

In early March 1996, the Ninth Circuit Court of Appeals, in the case of *Compassion in Dying v. State of Washington,* announced the discovery of a new "fundamental right" in the United States Constitution, a right to assisted suicide.

Finding Nonexistent Rights

It's amazing what can be seen with these new judicial microscopes, developed by the same people who made the Hubble telescope. It has been more than a century-and-a-quarter since passage of the Fourteenth Amendment and more than two centuries since the Bill of Rights, yet in all this time no one's eyesight was acute enough to discover this right. Using a high-powered judicial microscope, however, the Ninth Circuit was able to spot this marvelous constitutional provision: it's written in teeny-weeny letters, invisible to the naked eye, in the tail of one of the commas of the Fourteenth Amendment. (This is an improved version of the microscope used in 1973 by the Supreme Court when it discovered another fundamental right, abortion, which, we now know, had been inscribed in minute script in the upper portion of the same comma.)

Sad to say, three judges out of the court's eleven were not able to discern the right to suicide, despite the microscope. But this is the same proportion of the American population that fails to master any new technology, just under 30 percent. I bet these three judges don't know how to use ATM cards either.

Judge Stephen Reinhardt, who wrote the majority opinion, is not only a virtuoso at this new optico-juridical technology; he is also, it turns out, a great sociologist, able to assure us that "there is no reason to believe that legalizing assisted suicide will lead to the horrific consequences its opponents suggest."

Panicky people fear that constitutionalization of assisted suicide will lead to pressures on old people to speed up their deaths, pressures originating in some cases from impatient relatives but more often from cost-conscious health insurance providers, including government. These worrywarts have even coined a new name for the thing they fear: "seniorcide" or "elderly genocide."

Others worry that if assisted suicide is a "fundamental right" there will be no logical way to limit this right to a small number of hard cases, just as we cannot limit the right of abortion to hard cases. If something's a fundamental right, then it's a fundamental right; it should be available to everybody in virtually all circumstances.

Still others worry that making suicide a constitutional right is tantamount to declaring it a moral right, since in America that's the way we view constitutional rights; and that this "moralization" of suicide will increase its attractiveness and acceptability among the young.

Not to worry. Judge Reinhardt has turned sociology into a predictive science, something sociologists themselves have been trying to do, without success, for the last century-and-a-half. He has seen the future, and it works. It is a future in which assisted suicide is compassionate, rational, and tidy; in which everything else goes on as usual with this single happy exception—a few in desperate pain are allowed to make a voluntary exodus; a future, in short, in which the foolish decisions of the likes of Judge Reinhardt have no "horrific consequences."

Using Consistency Instead of Logic

At about this point somebody will object, "So you don't like the conclusion the Ninth Circuit has arrived at. So what? Your ridicule doesn't change the fact that the decision is judicially sound. It follows quite logically from Supreme Court precedents, especially *Roe v. Wade* (1973) and *Planned Parenthood v. Casey* (1992). There is a straight line from *Griswold v. Connecticut* (1965) to *Compassion in Dying*. Maybe you don't like it, but that's the way the system works."

> *"Using a high-powered judicial microscope the Ninth Circuit was able to spot [the right to assisted suicide] in teeny-weeny letters in . . . the Fourteenth Amendment."*

I confess to the sin of not being a lawyer, and to the even greater sin of not being a professor of constitutional law; but it seems to me there is something odd in the logic used by many American legal minds. In other fields of intellectual endeavor the *reductio ad absurdum* is recognized as a valid logical move: if your premises lead to absurd conclusions, there must be something wrong with your premises. But in constitutional law the opposite principle prevails: if your premises lead to absurdities (for example, that there are fundamental constitutional rights to abortion and assisted suicide), then you should lovingly embrace the conclusions and declare, despite appearances, that they are not the least bit absurd.

"A foolish consistency is the hobgoblin of little minds," said [poet Ralph Waldo] Emerson. He might have added, "—and of big judges." Normal people think common sense is entitled to trump consistency when the two conflict. Legal theorists of the Blackmun/Reinhardt persuasion think it works the other way round.

The Courts Are Destroying Themselves

I regret the flippant tone of this column, especially when speaking of one of the three grand divisions of the federal government. Respect for courts, above all the highest federal courts, is one of the great foundations of liberty and social order in this country, and I am reluctant to contribute to the erosion of this respect. My car does not sport one of those bumper stickers that says, "Question authority."

But what is one to do? It is not the critics who damage the legitimacy of courts so much as it is the courts who undermine their own legitimacy by inventing constitutional provisions that outrage both common sense and the moral feelings of vast numbers of Americans. When courts do this, how can we persuade ourselves to respect them? If you prick us, do we not bleed?

> *"Making suicide a constitutional right is tantamount to declaring it a moral right."*

And if we are told, "That's the way the system works," we answer that that's not the way the system was supposed to work at all. For these decisions are not only preposterous in content but undemocratic in method. In creating rights of suicide and abortion, judges—unelected aristocrats with life tenure—abolish rights of legislatures and the people who elect them. If homicidal rights are to be created at all, this should be done via the democratic process.

To be fair, however, it should be noted that in its graciousness the judiciary has allowed us to remain a democracy in a hundred small matters while reserving to itself the authority to decide only the really big questions. So don't worry. Democracy won't disappear entirely until the Supreme Court brings the method of filling potholes under the rubric of constitutional rights—and this won't happen for another twenty or thirty years at the earliest.

The Desire for Assisted Suicide Can Be Alleviated

by Burke J. Balch and Randall K. O'Bannon

About the authors: *Burke J. Balch is the director of the Department of Medical Ethics for the National Right to Life Committee. Randall K. O'Bannon is the director of the Department of Education for the National Right to Life Committee.*

Under the banners of compassion and autonomy, some are calling for legal recognition of a "right to suicide" and societal acceptance of "physician-assisted suicide." Suicide proponents evoke the image of someone facing unendurable suffering who calmly and rationally decides death is better than life in such a state. They argue that society should respect and defer to the freedom of choice such people exercise in asking to be killed. But what would be the consequences of accepting this perspective? Let us examine the facts.

Almost All Suicides Are Mentally Ill

Accepting a "right to suicide" would create a legal presumption of sanity, preventing appropriate mental health treatment. If suicide and physician-assisted suicide become legal rights, the presumption that people attempting suicide are deranged and in need of psychological help, borne out by many studies and years of experience, would be reversed. Those seeking suicide would be legally entitled to be left alone to do something irremediable, based on a distorted assessment of their circumstances, without genuine help.

An attempt at suicide, some psychologists say, is often a challenge to see if anyone out there really cares. Indeed, seeking physician assistance in a suicide, rather than just acting to kill oneself, may well be a manifestation, however subconscious, of precisely that challenge. If society creates a "right to suicide" and legalizes "physician-assisted suicide," the message perceived by a suicide attempter is not likely to be, "We respect your wishes," but rather, "we don't care if you live or die."

Almost all who commit suicide have mental health problems. Few people, if any, simply sit down and make a cool, rational decision to commit suicide. In

Reprinted from "Why We Shouldn't Legalize Assisting Suicide," by Burke J. Balch and Randall K. O'Bannon. Reprinted with permission. Article available at www.nrlc.org/euthanasia/asisuid1.html.

fact, studies have indicated that 93–94% of those committing suicide suffer from some identifiable mental disorder. In one such study, conducted by Dr. Eli Robbins of suicides occurring in St. Louis, Missouri, 47% of those committing suicide were diagnosed as suffering from either schizophrenic panic disorders or from affective disorders such as depressive disorders, dysthymic disorders, or bipolar disorder. An additional 25% suffered from alcoholism while another 15% had some recognizable but undiagnosed psychiatric disorder. 4% were found to have organic brain syndrome, 2% were schizophrenic, and 1% were drug addicts. The total of those with diagnosable mental disorders was 94%. An independent British study came up with a remarkably similar total figure, finding that 93% of those who commit suicide suffer from a diagnosable mental disorder.

Persons with mental disorders make distorted judgments. Suicide is often a desperate step taken by individuals who consider their problems so intractable as to make their situations hopeless. But experts in psychology recognize the evaluations these individuals make of their personal situations are flawed.

The suicidal person suffering from depression typically undergoes severe emotional and physical strain. This physical and emotional exhaustion impairs basic cognition, creates unwarranted self-blame, and generally lowers overall self esteem, all of which easily lead to distorted judgements. These effects also contribute to the sense of hopelessness that is the primary trigger of most suicidal behavior.

> *"Few people, if any, simply sit down and make a cool, rational decision to commit suicide."*

Studies have shown that during the period of their obsession with the idea of killing themselves, suicidal individuals tend to think in a very rigid, dichotomous way, seeing everything in "all or nothing" terms; they are unable to see any range of genuine alternatives. Many seem to be locked into automatic thoughts and responses, rather than accurately to understand and respond to their environment. Suicide attempters also tend to maximize their problems, minimize their achievements, and generally to ignore the larger context of their situations. They sometimes have inordinately unrealistic expectations of themselves. During the period of their disorders, these individuals usually see life as much more traumatic than it actually is and view temporary minor setbacks as major permanent ones.

Most People Who Attempt Suicide Are Ambivalent

Most of those attempting suicide are ambivalent; often, the attempt is a cry for help. Studies and descriptions of suicide attempters who were prevented from committing suicide by outside intervention (or in some cases, because the means used in the attempt did not take complete effect) demonstrate that most suicidal individuals have neither an unequivocal nor an irreversible determination to die. For example, one study conducted by two psychiatrists in Seattle, Washington, found 75% of the 96 suicide attempters they studied were actually quite ambivalent about their intentions to die. It is not actually a desire to die, but rather the desire to accomplish something by the attempt that drives the attempter to consider such a drastic option. Suicide is the means, not the end.

Often, suicide attempters are apparently seeking to establish some means of communication with significant persons in their lives or to test those persons' care and affection. Psychologists have concluded that other motives for attempting suicide include retaliatory abandonment (responding to a perceived abandonment by others with a revengeful "abandonment" of them through death), aggression turned inward, a search for control, manipulative guilt, punishment, escapism, frustration, or an attempt to influence someone else. Communication of these feelings—rather than death—is the true aim of the suicide attempter. This explains why, paradoxically but truthfully, many say after an obvious suicide attempt that they really didn't want to kill themselves. Psychiatrists have long advanced the opinion that underlying a suicidal person's ostensible wish to die is actually a wish to be rescued, so that a suicide attempt may quite accurately be described, not as a wish to "leave it all behind," but as a "cry for help." To allow or assist in a suicide, therefore, is not truly fully respecting a person's "autonomy" or honoring an individual's real wishes.

> *"Often suicide attempters are seeking to establish some means of communication with significant persons in their lives or to test those persons' . . . affection."*

The disorders leading many to attempt suicide are treatable. Depression can be treated. Alcoholism can be overcome. The difficult situations and circumstances of life which, at the moment, seem permanent and pervasive, often dissolve or resolve in time. The emotional and cognitive patterns of thought and emotion which cloud the suicide attempter's judgement and lead to feelings of utter despair and hopelessness, with proper psychiatric care, can be rechanneled in more rational, positive ways.

Crucial to such turnarounds is intervening to stop the suicide attempt and getting the attempter professional psychological assistance. Encouraging or validating the disturbed individual's feelings or misperceptions in fact makes it less likely the individual will get the help he or she needs and subconsciously probably wants.

Few of those rescued from suicide attempts try again. Proof that most individuals attempting suicide are ambivalent, temporarily depressed, and suffering from treatable disorders is the fact that so few, once rescued and treated, ever actually go on to commit suicide. In one American study, less than 4% of 886 suicide attempters actually went on to kill themselves in the 5 years following their initial attempt. A Swedish study published in 1977 of individuals who attempted suicide at some time between 1933 and 1942 found that only 10.9% of those eventually killed themselves in the subsequent 35 years. This suggests that intervention to keep an individual alive is actually the course most likely to honor that individual's true wishes or to respect the person's "autonomy."

People Should Strive for Life, Not Death

by Maurice Lamm

About the author: *Orthodox Rabbi Maurice Lamm is a rabbinics professor at Yeshiva University in New York City. He is a hospice care activist and the author of a number of books on Judaism, death, and hope, including* The Jewish Way of Death and Mourning.

We are toying with life and death again, and the flames of unintended consequences could blow the lid off society as we know it.

To the Valley of Dried Bones

Former Colorado Gov. Richard Lamm informed the seriously ill and elderly who need artificial life support that they have a "duty to die." Dr. Kevorkian performs his *suicide*-assistance in the back of old vans. An Internet site, called Deathnet, is where people chat about how best to die. Derek Humphrey's best-selling *Final Exit* provides prescriptions for over-the-counter death measures. All are train stops on the way down the slope to the valley of dried bones.

This eruption of humanitarian proposals has produced striking moral anomalies. It is simply bizarre that a handful of jurists, who base themselves on legalistic provincial judgments, take upon themselves decisions of such vast import for all of society. Many states have already legislated that planned suicide is a medical procedure despite the vociferous opposition of the very doctors who would assist the suicide. Of course, Health Maintenance Organizations, who own their doctors and jump at every opportunity to cut costs, will not pay for life-support machines. And, *mirabile dictu*, the public follows the lead of a few courts, who are usually conservative, over that of the American Medical Association, usually the paragons of plug-pulling.

Similar anomalies arose in surveys after publication of the hemlock book, *Final Exit.* They show that of the people who seek this option very few decide to do it because of overwhelming pain; that they are likely to be 60- to 80-year-olds who seek "a cool option" to "control their own destiny." It is positively

Reprinted from "The Right to Die and Duty to Live," by Maurice Lamm, *The Jewish Week*, October 11, 1996. Reprinted with permission from the author.

grotesque that a suicide manual could become a bestseller at the height of American prosperity.

And now Gov. Lamm. Why do old people have a duty to die? To enable fetuses and infants to "build a reasonable life" in a world of limited resources, and thereby to balance the budget. Business is business. A just-conceived fetus who has the brain of an amoeba and the personality of a slug has priority over an aging mother who broke her back and her heart, raising children for four decades. It is incomprehensible that millions of Americans nod obediently.

Dying to Die

You just cannot avoid the stunning paradox: we are the richest, freest, most ingenious people in history. But we won't spend a buck to keep the old lady alive. We have everything to live for, but we're dying to die.

Here is the catch that makes voluntary euthanasia especially insidious: it is carried out by decent people out of the goodness of their hearts. Now compassion is an obviously precious moral virtue. But beware of sweetness growing so widely that it strangles its host organism; it is grossly metastasized compassion. Eccelesiastes was counterintuitive: "Do not be over-righteous; do not be over-wise." This is exactly what makes the hemlock book so devilish and so attractive; why Kevorkian evokes disgust and heroism; and why Gov. Lamm becomes an object of derision and admiration. They are calls for death that issue straight from the heart of pity. Kindness run amok. Out of empathy come the most dispassionate, dangerous solutions; from the nicest people come the ugliest answers; death springs from love; Thanatos from Eros.

Judaism, and all the Western world's religions that derive from it, knew better, much better. They resolutely said "No!" to the "sweet death" of euthanasia.

The first imperative of life is: live. Judaism not only frowned on suicide; it positively outlawed it. It raged against the idea of taking a guiltless life, which can be reclaimed only by its author, God. A person is a spiritual being, a creation of God. Taking a life through euthanasia is killing, regardless of the spin you put on it. You cannot measure the worth of anyone's life, including your own. Mathematics and mortality walk hand-in-hand here. If life is infinitely holy, a fraction of life is also infinitely holy.

A dying person, no matter his condition, is alive in all respects; no person is "dead" before he dies. He must be treated with full human dignity. In inhuman conditions, we must be

> *"[These events in the assisted suicide movement] all are train stops on the way down the slope to the valley of dried bones."*

more human. That's the meaning of "death with dignity." It is morally obligatory to use all means to ease suffering—even heroin. In certain circumstances of impending death or irreversible brain-stem damage or the absence of independent respiration, "letting die" might be an option. Inserting tubes and being tethered to machines often only prolongs dying, not living. But despite the agony and the often tragic uselessness, "making die" is not an option God ever gives to human beings. Lord knows the time of terminal illness is a family's most devastating trial. But we may under no circumstances put innocent human beings to death, even "for their own good."

The Jewish Commitment to Life

The Jewish edge in human history comes in part through its commitment to life in every conceivable situation. Life goes on—even when life becomes hell. It would have been simple to surrender to death in the old ghetto. We didn't need instructions in a book. Instead, Jews struggled on. When the Rebbe [Rabbi] of Breslav heard the people begging to end it all, he cried out, "Gevalt Yiden! Don't surrender!" and then etched those words over the portals of the synagogue. Crisis triggered courage, not a glut of opinions. The Jews survived because they had a duty to live. They knew it as a divine commandment, "He shall live by them." Jewish doctors were as compassionate as Kevorkian, but his radical solution was not even thinkable. Life before all else, even before death.

> *"We have everything to live for, but we're dying to die."*

The answer to the desperation of dying lies in compassion and courage and understanding, and even hope in "hopeless" circumstances. Not suicide. Kevorkian is wrong, dead wrong, even if the circumstances of some individual's dying are horrendous in the extreme. The "sweet death" of hemlock is a denial of life and all it embraces. Hemlock is not a Jewish flower.

As for the morally-challenged governor, from this Lamm to that Lamm: We have no duty to die. Ever. We do have a right to die. Sometimes. But we have a duty to live. Always. Everybody.

Physicians Should Not Be Involved with Suicide

by Anneke Quinta

About the author: *Anneke Quinta is a resident in family practice at Kingston Hospital in New York.*

"Help me to die," she said. I looked down at Margaret in surprise. The witty Welsh woman had been my patient for several weeks. A veteran of our surgical unit, she had weathered several major operations and now faced another. Usually optimistic, she shared my opinion that this hospital stay would be her last.

Margaret's request seemed reasonable. Her mind was clear. She understood her deteriorating condition and concluded that the best thing I could do for her was to end her life. She had a terminal illness and wanted to spare herself and her family the pain of prolonged suffering. She was competent to make a decision and clearly stated her wish.

Over the ensuing weeks, Margaret's pain grew worse. One by one, conventional methods of pain relief failed, and my feelings of inadequacy increased. Margaret often asked me to help her die. Faced with her request, I could no longer skirt the issue. Should doctors help patients like her commit suicide? Many consider physician-assisted suicide the ultimate in personal choice. With a few guidelines, they believe, Margaret and others like her could have their wish. A recent University of Michigan study offers three guidelines. First, the patient must be a mentally competent adult whose death is expected within six months. Second, the patient must request her physician's assistance to end her life on more than one occasion. Third, a second physician must examine the patient and agree with the diagnosis and outlook. The study found that 66 percent of the public and 56 percent of the physicians surveyed favored the legalization of physician-assisted suicide if such guidelines were used.[1]

Do we know what we are choosing? Perhaps we can learn from the Netherlands, a nation where similar guidelines are already in effect. To determine how well the system was working, the Dutch government collected data on 8,100

Reprinted from " The Assisted Suicide Debate," by Anneke Quinta, *Plough,* no. 52, Summer 1997. Reprinted by permission of *Plough.*

cases in which doctors prescribed lethal overdoses of medication. They found that 61 percent of the patients had not consented to their death.[2] Doctors defended their actions by saying they did what they believed the patient or the patient's family wanted. However, in 45 percent of these cases, doctors didn't even consult family members.[3]

"In one [recent legal case], a psychiatrist helped a depressed but physically healthy patient commit suicide."

Two recent legal cases further show that abuse occurs despite regulations. In one, a psychiatrist helped a depressed but physically healthy patient commit suicide without treating the depression. The court merely reprimanded the doctor, saying his action undermined faith in the medical profession. In another case, a gynecologist gave a fatal injection to a severely handicapped baby. The appeals court ruled that the doctor made a "justified choice."

Physician-Assisted Suicide and the Holocaust

Why have the Dutch fallen so disastrously short of complying with their own guidelines, despite the "advanced" environment provided by their modern healthcare and legal systems? Are they an exception or the rule? Consider this excerpt from a *New York Times* article:

> The memorandum . . . proposed that "it shall be made possible for physicians to end the tortures of incurable patients, upon request, in the interests of true humanity." Incurability would be determined not only by the attending physician, but also by two official doctors who would carefully trace the history of the case and personally examine the patient . . . the patient himself shall "expressly and earnestly" ask it, or "in case the patient no longer is able to express his desire, his nearer relatives, acting from motives that do not contravene morals, shall so request."[4]

This rhetoric sounds like something from the current debate on physician-assisted suicide, and the guidelines it proposes are similar to those favored by a majority of today's physicians and the public. Yet the article is from 1933, and the memorandum it quotes was issued by none other than Hitler's German Justice Ministry.

The outcome of this memorandum warrants further examination. The German Medical Association set up a system to implement the proposal, legalizing physician-assisted suicide. Doctors started on competent patients with terminal illnesses who requested it, then mentally incompetent patients, and eventually anyone economically—or ideologically—unprofitable to the state. Between 1933 and 1941, over seventy thousand "futile or terminal" patients were killed *in German hospitals.*

To the State, the main benefit of the "T4 Euthanasia Program," as it came to be known, was economic. It saved 88 million Reichmarks per year.[5] The program was "geared toward economic performance in the healthcare market and cost efficient utilization of limited resources."[6] (Sound like a contemporary medical economics journal?) To increase efficiency, the Nazis moved the technology developed in the T4 killing hospitals to specialized centers—death camps.

For many in our society today, the premise that certain human lives are not worth saving is not a shocking one. It may be a well-guarded one, hidden by euphemisms and denied under fire; nonetheless, it underlies widespread approval of physician-assisted suicide, and this is why the historical lesson applies to our situation. . . . Call me an alarmist, but as far as I can see, a dangerously similar combination of the factors in play in Germany during the 1930s influences American healthcare today.

Public opinion favors physician-assisted suicide, and court rulings mirror this. The Ninth Circuit Court of Appeals recently overturned Washington State's ban on physician-assisted suicide, saying the "right to determine the time and manner of one's death" outweighed the state's duty to preserve life.[7] "Quality of life" has replaced the time-honored concept of "sanctity of life."

Powerful managed care companies, obsessed with efficient resource utilization, now control much of healthcare. Increasingly, cost seems to influence the care of the dying more than anything else. Without quality medical care available and affordable for all, the poor may soon be forced to "choose" suicide instead of costly extended care. It is easy to see how the "right" to die could become a death sentence for the most vulnerable.

> *"The 'right' to die could become a death sentence for the most vulnerable."*

So what of Margaret? It is clear to me that given its track record—historical and contemporary—we can never allow physician-assisted suicide in our country. It is also clear to me, as a Christian, that no one has a right to assist another in taking her own life or in deciding the hour of death. All the more, we must meet the challenge of making dying as positive and comfortable an experience as possible.

As doctors, nurses, and care providers, we must provide more than healthcare, and as families we must provide more than money. But we must also do more, and we can start on a very simple, personal level. We must make our patients, our relatives, our elderly neighbors, and our colleagues feel so wanted and needed that they will not want to die. Instead of shunning the dying or making them feel (however subtly) that they are a burden on us, we must surround them with love. When this happens, will assisted suicide still be an issue?

Notes

1. J.G. Bachman et al., "Attitudes of Michigan Physicians and Public Toward Legalizing Physician Assisted Suicide." *NEJM* 1996; 334:303–09.

2. *Medical Decisions About the End of Life* (transl. from the Dutch). The Hague, Netherlands: SDU, 1991.

3. *U.S. News & World Report,* April 25, 1994, 36.

4. *New York Times*, Oct. 8, 1933.

5. *Medizin im Nationalsozialismus: Ein Arbeitsbuch.* Tübingen, Germany: Schwäbische Verlagsgesellschaft, 1980, 25.

6. Hartmut M. Hanauske-Abel, "Not a Slippery Slope or Sudden Subversion: German Medicine and National Socialism in 1933." *BMJ* 1996; 313: 1453–63.

7. George J. Annas, "The Promised End: Constitutional Aspects of Physician-Assisted Suicide." *NEJM* 1996; 335:683–87.

Chapter 4

How Can Suicide Be Prevented?

Suicide Prevention: An Overview

by David Lester

About the author: *David Lester is professor of psychology at The Richard Stockton College of New Jersey and the author of over 1,000 articles and 60 books on the subjects of suicide and murder.*

Because suicidal behavior can occur anywhere, anytime and to anyone, it is essential that everyone have, at the very least, a basic understanding of suicide, its warning signs and how to respond when confronted with a situation of this sort. Of course, some people are able to come to grips with their problems on their own, but most suicidal people want and need help from others to help solve their problems, or at least to help get through a suicidal crisis.

The Role of Family and Friends

The most convenient and potentially most useful sources of help for the suicidal person are his friends and family. These people are usually available, they have considerable knowledge of the suicidal person's past history and it doesn't cost anything to talk to them. In addition, comfort and counsel from friends and relatives cannot be interpreted by the suicidal person as "paid friendship," as the relationship with a professional therapist sometimes is. If friends and relatives are sensitive to the behavior of the suicidal person and aware of the basic facts about suicide, they may be able to help save a life. There are a number of ideas that friends and families should keep in mind when dealing with potential suicides.

If you believe that a person may be suicidal, there are steps you can take to help that person communicate his feelings to you. In addition to providing the potential suicide with an emotional outlet, you may also be able to help him with his problems and, at the same time, determine the degree of suicidal intent.

Listen actively. Suicidal people are often confused about what they want and how to get it. They have a need and they feel pain and they try to communicate these feelings to another person. Often they need help in clarifying confusing feelings. Sometimes this can be done by talking with them about their feelings (both those they express verbally and those they communicate by gestures or facial expressions). They may be able to better understand their own feelings simply by talking to someone and hearing themselves talk. . . .

Do not be afraid to ask direct questions such as, "Do you feel so bad that you are considering suicide?" At one time or another, most people have considered suicide, even if it was just a fleeting thought. Do not worry that you might actually be giving the person the idea of committing suicide. In fact, bringing the subject out into the open can often be an enormous relief to the suicidal person who desperately wants to discuss his feelings and even specifically his suicidal plans, but is worried about scaring and alienating you. When you take the initiative and raise the question directly, it shows that you are taking the person seriously and that you are responding to his pain.

Try to determine the degree of suicidal intent. By asking a suicidal person questions about important issues, you will not only be able to determine the seriousness of his suicidal intent, but you will also encourage him to discuss his feelings. In addition, such questions let the potential suicide know that you are taking him seriously. If the answer is "Yes, I am considering suicide," you may ask him which method of suicide he is considering, does he have the means, has he decided when to do it and has he ever tried suicide before. The answers to these questions will allow you to determine the seriousness of his suicidal intent. You should also ask yourself how lethal is his plan, how available are the means and when you think he might act. Friends should not let social delicacy deter them from discussing specific details about suicidal behavior. It is a myth that talking about suicide to distressed individuals can encourage them to kill themselves. It is important to take the person's overall response into consideration when interpreting his answer; a very distressed person may say he is not suicidal even when he is. If you suspect this is the case, it may be helpful to ask him what he would do if he ever did feel suicidal.

Do not leave the person alone if the level of suicidal intent seems very high. If you believe that a person is seriously suicidal and may harm himself in the very near future, do *not* leave him alone. Even seemingly harmless activities, such as a trip to the bathroom, are opportunities for a person in the midst of a severe crisis to hurt himself.

> **"The most convenient and potentially most useful sources of help for the suicidal person are his friends and family."**

Seek professional help and follow through. You will probably be able to most help the person if you do whatever you can to refer him to a professional for evaluation and treatment. Do not leave it up to him to seek help; follow through, not only by making sure that arrangements have been made to see someone, but also by making sure he gets there. Even if you are sworn to secrecy, remember that this is not a test of friendship but a cry for help. If you don't feel equipped to do this alone, find another person to help you or turn it over to someone else. If you don't know where to turn, look in the telephone directory for a 24-hour telephone counseling or suicide prevention service in your area. If the crisis is acute, call 911, a suicide hotline, or take the person to a hospital emergency room or a walk-in clinic at a psychiatric hospital.

Professional Help

Although friends and family can be instrumental in aiding suicidal people, it must be recognized that there are times when this kind of intervention is not enough. For cases in which friends and relatives are themselves contributing to the disturbance that is causing a person distress and making him feel suicidal, the only person who may be able to offer help is someone outside of this tangle of unhappy relationships. As well, friends and relatives may be temperamentally unsuited to dealing with this kind of difficult problem; they may become impatient or agitated in spite of having the best intentions. They may even have reason to benefit from the person's suicide. Finally, a suicidal person may be seriously disturbed and in a state that cannot be addressed by a nonprofessional.

In such cases there are a number of resources to which potential suicides and those concerned about them can turn. First there are psychologists and other mental health professionals who can provide counseling and psychotherapy and psychiatrists who can prescribe appropriate medication. The majority of suicidal people are depressed and today there are a variety of effective antidepressants, such as Prozac for depressive disorders, and lithium for those with bipolar affective disorders. There are also effective short-term cognitive therapies for helping depressed suicidal clients, as well as family therapy and group therapy for these clients and their families.

> *"It is a myth that talking about suicide to distressed individuals can encourage them to kill themselves."*

It is important to make sure that the professional you turn to for help is comfortable with the issue of suicide; many therapists do not like to deal with suicide cases and try to avoid accepting them as clients. The anxiety connected with the possibility of a client's suicide may be overwhelming for the therapist. If possible, therefore, it is wise to choose a therapist or counselor who has experience with suicidal people and who feels at ease accepting them as clients. Crisis intervention and suicide prevention centers can provide information about which therapists and counselors in the community are best suited for counseling suicidal clients. . . .

Suicide Prevention Groups and Crisis Centers

In most communities in the United States, and in Australia, Canada, the United Kingdom and western Europe, there are suicide organizations whose purpose is to prevent suicide and to advance its study. Generally, the goals of most of these organizations are to: support research projects that attempt to understand and treat depression; provide information and education about depression and suicide both to the general public, survivors and those plagued with depression and suicide; promote professional education for the recognition and treatment of depressed and suicidal individuals; publicize the magnitude of the problems of depression and suicide and the need for research, prevention and treatment; and to support programs for survivor treatment, research and education.

> *"Many suicide prevention specialists argue that if lethal means are not readily available when a person decides to attempt suicide, it may affect the outcome."*

Most of these organizations offer many different services, a general breakdown of which follows:

School Gatekeeper Training: This type of program is directed at school staff (teachers, counselors, coaches, etc.) to help identify students at risk of suicide and refer such students to appropriate help. These programs also teach staff how to respond to crises such as a sudden death of a classmate.

Community Gatekeeper Training: This type of gatekeeper program provides training to community members (clergy, police, merchants, recreation staff and physicians, nurses and other clinicians). This training is designed to help people identify at-risk youths and refer them as appropriate.

General Suicide Education: These programs provide students with facts about suicide, alert them to suicide warning signs and provide information on how to seek help for themselves and others. These programs often incorporate a variety of self-esteem or social competency development activities.

Screening Programs: Screening involves the administration of an instrument to identify high-risk youth in order to provide more targeted assessment and treatment. Repeated administration of the screening instrument can also be used to measure changes in attitudes or behavior over time, to test the effectiveness of an employed prevention strategy and to obtain early warning signs of potential suicidal behavior.

Peer Support Programs: These programs, which can be conducted in school or nonschool settings, are designed to foster peer relationships, competency development and social skills among youth at high risk of suicide.

Crisis Centers and Hotlines: These programs primarily provide telephone counseling for suicidal people. Hotlines are usually staffed by trained volunteers. Some of them also have a "drop in" crisis center and offer referrals.

Intervention after a Suicide: Strategies have been developed to cope with the potential crisis of suicide clusters that sometimes occur after a suicide occurs. They are designed in part to help prevent or contain suicide clusters and to help youth effectively cope with feelings of loss that come with the sudden death or suicide of a peer. Preventing further suicide is but one of the several goals of interventions made with friends and relatives of a suicide victim. . . .

These centers often operate in very different ways, but their members have in common a special regard for the problems of suicidal people and special training for dealing with them. In some countries, all the suicide prevention centers are administered and supervised by one group. In the United Kingdom, for example, all of the centers are run by an organization called The Samaritans, a nonreligious charity that has been offering emotional support to suicidal persons for over 40 years by phone, visit and letter. (The Samaritans are based in England, but they are an international organization.) They state that "callers are guaranteed absolute confidentiality and retain the right to make their own decisions including the decision to end their life." In the United States, each center is independent and although many meet the standards established by the American Association of Suicidology, there is no single model for how these centers operate. . . .

The primary service offered by most suicide prevention centers is a 24-hour telephone hotline, often advertised under different names such as suicide prevention, teen hotline, crisis intervention and problems in living. The rationale for crisis hotlines relies on the idea that suicide attempts are often precipitated by a stressful event, that they are often impulsive and are usually contemplated with ambivalence. Hotline counselors are designed to respond to the crisis, deter the caller from hurting himself and working with him until the crisis has passed. Hotlines offer an immediately available source of help; they do not require travel to a clinic; and they are anonymous, allowing callers the opportunity to be open without fear of harsh judgment.

> *"The taboo against taking one's own life is so deeply ingrained that the direct discussion of suicide is often avoided."*

At least one worker is always at the center to talk to the people who call in to discuss their problems. During the hours when demand is heavy, there may be four or five counselors available. Australia's Lifeline centers have a toll-free number. If all of the telephone counselors at one center are occupied with clients, the caller is automatically switched to an available counselor at a neighboring center. In some centers, a professional staff and trained lay counselors take the telephone calls during the day and volunteers take them in the evenings, at night and on weekends.

Some centers accommodate walk-in clients for face-to-face counseling and a number of them have established groups to help people who have attempted suicide as well as those who have lost a loved one to suicide (usually called survivors). Because the main purpose of these centers is to assist people in crisis, most of them do not take on clients for long-term therapy; to do so would tie up the counseling staff, making them unavailable for responding to new clients who are in crisis and need immediate help. Therefore, when clients seem to need long-term counseling, they are usually referred to other agencies in the community or the surrounding area. . . .

School Suicide and Death Education Programs

In recent years, many school systems have incorporated death education and suicide intervention and prevention programs into their curricula, a development that is, in large part, in response to the enormous rise in adolescent suicide in the past few decades. Many of these programs can assist parents who need help (for their children or themselves), often by referring them to appropriate agencies and support groups in the area. Many people and groups have criticized these programs because they feel that they upset students who are depressed and possibly suicidal and that they are not able to prevent suicide. Others believe that the programs are important and have been successful in achieving their goals. Unfortunately, aside from the educational programs for school students, little other effort has been made to inform the general public about suicide. Perhaps as more and more people become aware of the pervasiveness and seriousness of the problem, they will seek out information on their own and make sure they learn how to respond to suicidal behavior. . . .

The Internet

Fortunately, there is now a good deal of information available on the Internet that is immediately available to anyone with a computer. Almost all of the suicide and crisis intervention organizations have websites whose varied offerings include: excellent and detailed information on critical issues such as warning signs, what to do and what not to do when faced with a person's suicidal crisis; answers to frequently asked questions; phone numbers of crisis hotlines and addresses of organizations; a comprehensive listing of support groups in your community and on the Internet; links to more specific information; and listings of useful books, articles and journals. Some of them even offer online counseling, many of them respond daily to Email letters and there are also quite a few electronic self-help support groups where people can talk to each other about their suicidal feelings, thoughts, intentions or previous attempts in a safe, emotionally supportive environment. Other Internet resources are mailing lists and newsgroups which are forums of discussion for people who work in or who are interested in the fields of suicide prevention and crisis counseling, or who themselves are suicidal. . . .

Restricting Access to Methods for Suicide

Because impulsiveness appears to play an important role in suicide (especially among young people), and because ambivalence is a typical characteristic of suicides (i.e., the decision to go through with the act waxes and wanes), many suicide prevention specialists argue that if lethal means are not readily available when a person decides to attempt suicide, it may affect the outcome in several ways. First, it may delay the attempt, allowing the person to later decide against suicide. Second, it may prompt the person to use a less lethal means, therefore allowing for a greater chance that he may be saved. Furthermore, there is the possibility that some attempts would never be acted on if substantial effort was needed to arrange for the method of suicide.

We can see what happens when lethal means are restricted by the following incident. In England, in the 1960s and 1970s, during the time that the domestic gas industry switched from coal gas (containing highly toxic carbon monoxide) to natural gas (containing less toxic methane), the English suicide rate declined by about 30 percent. This suggests that many people who would have used gas to kill themselves apparently did not switch to another method when their preference became unavailable.

The emission controls on cars, instituted to reduce pollution, have also made exhaust fumes less toxic and therefore less likely to cause death. Another way to make it harder for people to poison and kill themselves with carbon monoxide from cars would be for manufacturers to install a device that would automatically turn off the engine after it idled for a few minutes. Also, to make it harder to attach a hose to the exhaust pipes of cars, manufacturers could change the shape of the pipes from round to flat and wide.

Clarke and Lester documented the many ways in which easy access to lethal methods for suicide, such as firearms, increases their use for suicide. They urged such tactics as placing limits on the sale and ownership of firearms; fencing in bridges and high buildings from which people jump; restricting the availability of poisonous fertilizers and insecticides in developing countries where they are often used to commit suicide; as well as reducing the number of pills that doctors prescribe and the prescription of less toxic medications.

It would seem particularly important to restrict ready access to firearms. Nearly two-thirds of all suicides among males aged 15 to 24 are committed with guns. Unlike drug ingestion and carbon monoxide poisoning, a suicide attempt with a firearm is often immediately lethal, leaving very little opportunity for rescue.

Critics have argued that if people have trouble obtaining the means of first choice for suicide, they will simply find another method. Clarke and Lester replied that many suicidal people have a specific preferred method for suicide and would not switch. If they do switch, they may have to use a less lethal method. Furthermore, because the suicidal state is often a crisis state that can pass in a very short

> *"The question sometimes arises whether it is appropriate to try to prevent the suicide in all circumstances."*

while, if it is difficult for a person to quickly find a lethal alternative, by the time he finally obtains the means for committing suicide, the suicidal crisis may be past.

The strategy of restricting access to methods for committing suicide is frequently used in hospitals and prisons to prevent patients and inmates from taking their lives. A great deal of thought has been given to how to make rooms and cells "suicide-proof." In correctional facilities, not only should surveillance be intensified for inmates who seem suicidal, but also every effort should be made to restrict suicidal inmates' access to dangerous items that could be used for suicide.

Restricting access to lethal methods would not necessarily reduce suicide attempts, but it certainly has the potential for preventing suicides.

Why Prevent Suicide?

In the same way that most people believe that the prolongation of life is always desirable over death, most people also assume that the prevention of suicide is always the right avenue of thought. Most people regard life as sacred. Reverence for life is a part of many religions; even when it is separated from theological tenets, this belief remains deeply ingrained in most everyone. A murderer is looked upon with horror, and the people who deny the importance of life by killing themselves are often considered insane or evil. The taboo against taking one's own life is so deeply ingrained that the direct discussion of suicide is often avoided. This avoidance may extend even to the distortion of the actual cause of death on a suicide's death certificate.

In addition to these deep-rooted feelings about the value of life, there are many objective reasons for preventing suicide. Persons whose suicide attempts are thwarted are often grateful for being saved, and they shudder at the idea that they might actually have died. Those who call a suicide prevention center are clearly ambivalent about dying or else they wouldn't have called; they are asking for alternative solutions to their problem. If a person commits suicide, his survivors usually suffer terribly. Not only are they deprived of the companionship and perhaps the financial support of their loved one, but they may also experience great guilt and distress because they are afraid that they contributed to the suicide's problems or at least failed to save him. In cultures where suicide is considered highly taboo, the family may feel disgraced. Children whose parent commits suicide may be tormented by the notion that they might have inherited suicidal tendencies.

Finally, many people choose suicide as a solution to problems in their lives and they see death as the only way to escape when in actuality there are other ways of coping. If we save them, we can give them another chance to work through their difficulties. The successful and permanent prevention of suicide involves correction of the problems that are leading people toward suicide, thus making them happier and more productive, rather than simply keeping them alive.

In spite of all these good reasons for the prevention of suicide, the question sometimes arises whether it is appropriate to try to prevent the suicide in all circumstances. Many suicidologists would say that prevention efforts are always appropriate. Existentialists, on the other hand, would contend that suicide may sometimes be a healthy act. In 1958, Binswanger, an existential psychiatrist, said of one of his patients that he believed that suicide was the only healthy, free, mature and responsible action she could take. Most suicide experts would not go so far as to advocate suicide because of its existential advantages. However, when a person is seriously preoccupied with suicide for a long period of time and therefore requires constant observation and guarding (perhaps in the locked ward of a psychiatric hospital), we must ask ourselves whether compromising his dignity and humanity is not more damaging to the quality of his life as a whole than the possibility that his life will end in suicide.

This issue is especially relevant today because more and more people who are suffering from chronic terminal illnesses such as AIDS are deciding that they would rather die by suicide than live a life with so much suffering. There are books in print that explain how to kill oneself quickly and relatively painlessly and physicians who are willing to help. Dr. Kevorkian has even designed a poison-dispensing "suicide machine" for people who want to die. Some people rationally decide to commit suicide, feeling that death (both subjectively and objectively) is preferable to further life. In certain circumstances, suicide may appear to be the best possible solution to an impossible situation. As people have different styles of life, so each, it could be argued, should have the right to his own style of death. For some individuals, death by suicide may be the most appropriate end to life.

> *"As people have different styles of life, so each, it could be argued, should have the right to his own style of death."*

In strong disagreement, Shneidman and his colleagues argued that even severely ill persons should be discouraged from committing suicide because "while there is life, there is hope" and also because their deaths will cause so much guilt in survivors. Similarly, Richman feels that rather than acquiescing in the suicidal deaths of patients with chronic and terminal illnesses, we should make strenuous efforts to improve the quality of their final months or years of life.

In response to Shneidman's point, it is rather rare for a person approaching death to be totally cured and able to return to a normal life. And as for the guilt of relatives, it would be more realistic to say that guilt should be experienced by those who insist on forcing a loved one to maintain an unwanted and painful life. A survivor's severe guilt over the suicide of a gravely ill relative may be pathological or deserved because he treated that person unfairly. In either case, the guilt is not an event within the life of the dying person and he is the one who should be our chief concern.

We should realize that the quality of life can sometimes be more important than its quantity. There are times when people should not be subjected to prolonged agony followed by inevitable death simply on the grounds that no matter what, "life is sacred."

Encouraging Teens to Talk May Prevent Suicide

by Rebecca Blumenstein

About the author: *Rebecca Blumenstein is a former staff writer for* Newsday *and currently a reporter for the* Wall Street Journal.

They trickled into classrooms at Elwood's John Glenn High School clutching sleeping bags, pillows, teddy bears and Pearl Jam CDs.

It was Friday night. But not any normal Friday night for these 80 teenagers. There would be no basketball games. No parties. No movies. And no complaining how little there is to do on Long Island this night.

With the encouragement of "Doc," school psychologist Anthony Pantaleno, they split into groups of 20 for an overnight encounter designed to explore teenage angst in the '90s—and perhaps intervene in troubled lives before they self-destruct.

"I want you to think of yourselves as precious people, because you are," said Pantaleno, dressed in a Hawaiian shirt and bright yellow shorts instead of his traditional jacket and tie. Scanning the group, a broad mix of students who had volunteered for the weekend or had been strongly encouraged to come, he said: "You need to understand you are not alone and we are there to help."

And then he showed them why. He dimmed the lights and told the group to move all the desks to the side and spread out their sleeping bags to get comfortable, a strange sight in a classroom whose walls were consumed with Shakespeare's "MacBeth." He told them that they were going to sit in one place for at least three hours and talk about nothing other than what was happening in their lives. It started slowly, but one by one the students started talking, often swallowing tears between words.

"In school, people fall for my stupid jokes," one student said in the darkness, explaining that she acts funny to hide what she feels inside. "I am always lonely. I have no one to talk to. When I tell anyone I'm suicidal, they take it as a joke."

"As I got older, the pressures seemed to mount," said another. "I started slashing my arms. It didn't get any attention. . . . I still have some scars."

By the time the lights went up, almost half the teenagers in one group of 20 had confessed to having made either a gesture or serious attempt to end their lives.

Suddenly, the teenagers seemed aged beyond their years. They were lurching toward adulthood, but still clinging to childhood. One girl held a ragged childhood teddy bear she still sleeps with every night as she spoke about sophisticated psychological concepts such as co-dependency and alienation. Another boy played a Pearl Jam song on a CD player, saying it had saved his life during a breakup with a girlfriend who no longer spoke to him.

> *"Experts say that for every completed suicide there are hundreds of gestures or serious attempts that go unreported."*

Some might be shocked by the teenagers' depth of pain and the numbers of them who say they consider suicide in moments of desperation. But Pantaleno and the other professionals who conducted Elwood's "Awareness Weekend" weren't surprised. They point to several national studies that say as many as 90 percent of all teenagers think about suicide at one time or another. Though very few actually do it, experts say the numbers reflect a phenomenon that is particularly disturbing in suburbia.

State health department figures show, for example, that suicide rates for people between ages 15 and 24 is routinely higher in Nassau and Suffolk than in New York City. In recent years, Suffolk County has reported the highest numbers of suicides among young people of any county in the state. Experts theorize that one factor may be the isolation many teenagers feel in such a large county that is both densely suburban and rural.

In recent years, an average of 35 people between 15 and 24 have committed suicide annually on Long Island, and experts say that for every completed suicide there are hundreds of gestures or serious attempts that go unreported. In most cases, even successful suicides are hidden from public view. When two high school girls laid down on the railroad tracks in Setauket last December, it was a dramatic and highly publicized example of teenage suicide. But it was indicative of the more private suicides by young people that occur several times a month on Long Island.

Though suicide, of course, is not a problem unique to teenagers, psychologists and educators note that young people may be more likely to make rash decisions to end their own lives in moments of panic. State and national figures indicate there has been a slow but steady rise in teenage suicides since the mid 1980s—to 4,751 nationally, or 13 a day, in 1991, the last year for which figures are available. Suicide is the third leading cause of death of young people, behind homicide and traffic accidents. And experts say young people seem to be attempting suicide at younger ages than ever before—as young as 12 or 13, some report. Studies show teenage suicide cuts across economic lines but is much more frequent among whites than other racial groups.

In response, some high schools on Long Island and across the country have begun offering overnight retreats and other innovative programs in an attempt to help troubled teenagers.

At John Glenn, where officials say there have been no suicides in recent memory, Pantaleno and his colleagues decided to come at suicide indirectly. Most sessions in this month's overnight "Awareness Weekend" were geared to help students deal with major issues like substance abuse, loss and relationships—any of which can unravel the most balanced high school student. Modeled after a similar program started by Bay Shore High School, the weekend was open to all students. Some, including many who serve as "peer counselors," volunteered. Others were recruited by Pantaleno, who felt it was crucial to reach those most in need of help.

The participants represented a cross section of the school, some who are on the way to Ivy League schools and others who are on the verge of flunking out, those from wealthy households and those whose families are struggling to keep their homes.

The students were divided into four "family groups" designed to break down the cliques that form the backbone of this and virtually every high school: the jocks, the brains, the

"Psychologists and educators note that young people may be more likely to make rash decisions to end their own lives in moments of panic."

nerds, the burn-outs and, these days, the skateboarders and the hippy "granolas."

After some get-acquainted exercises, they were asked to write a few anonymous words about how they felt about the weekend encounter, in which they would meet almost continuously from the last bell on Friday afternoon until a square dance on Saturday night. Most said they were excited but nervous. Some said they felt nothing at all. Two wrote they felt "like dying."

"There are a lot of different groups in this room. When we pass each other in the halls, we wear our masks," said Pantaleno, as he began the weekend's most intense session Friday night, called "Sharing." "Tonight, we're going to try to take some of those masks off."

The students spoke about feeling alone in the world, about relentless academic pressures that parents often place on them. Some said it seemed like the only thing they could control was what they ate, a feeling that had led them into eating disorders like anorexia and bulimia. They spoke about the parental divorces that almost half of them had weathered, and how some have grown estranged from one or both parents after a remarriage. They spoke about coming home to empty houses, about seeing parents lose their jobs. And they spoke about how despite it all, no one seemed to acknowledge their pain.

"I gained weight and then I lost weight," one student said. "No matter which way I went I got criticized. Then someone used me. . . . I just started tearing myself up, cutting myself."

After each student spoke, the others wiggled their fingers in the air—applause in sign language. Sometimes, there were long silences, but then someone piped up with a story that seemed to erupt from deep inside. Though the students barely knew each other, they shared deeply held secrets. One boy confessed to having an obsessive-compulsive disorder. Some seemed overwhelmed at the numbers of their peers who had considered ending their lives. Only three of the 20 never said a word.

"There is nothing more sobering than when you hear one, after the other, after the other," said one of the professionals at the retreat, Don Pratt, recalling the first time he heard a group of teenagers relate thoughts of suicide. Pratt is director of community outreach for Response of Suffolk, which provides suicide counseling to schools.

Some skeptics might point out that teenagers always have problems, always feel they are growing up in an age of despair. Others say that kids today are simply more conscious and verbal about their problems because they are the products of a baby-boom generation that has defined itself by talking about its anxieties. But suicide experts say that although it's never been easy to grow up, it may be more difficult these days than ever before. Facing all the social ills of the 1990s, including alcoholism and drug abuse and an increasingly violent society, young people may have less adult support than ever before, in part because many have two working parents.

"Parents are so pressured with their lives right now that kids are more on their own," said Steven Spivak, an adolescent psychologist in Huntington who works with the Merrick school system. "Now it seems that adults are out of the picture too much."

And to hear some teenagers tell it, some parents don't pay enough attention, or minimize their children's emotional pain.

"I've been troubled before, and people say, 'You're fifteen. What kind of problems could you have? These are the best years of your life,'" said one sophomore, during a break at John Glenn. "That's enough to make anyone consider suicide right there."

Her friend agreed that there are misperceptions, especially in suburbia. "We're all supposed to be rich kids with no problems," she said. "That's not the case at all."

> *"The students spoke about feeling alone in the world, about relentless academic pressures that parents often place on them."*

One sophomore offered her own case during one session. She stood up and told her peers that her troubles had started in seventh grade, when her parents split up and she had to change schools. She began smoking marijuana to gain acceptance and quickly moved to other drugs before her parents caught on and threatened to kick her out of the house if she didn't get help. She enrolled in a drug-rehabilitation program and resumed school this year. "My parents caught me before it got real bad," she said. "Now, I'm just trying to stay straight and stay in high school. That's it."

> *"Suicide experts say that although it's never been easy to grow up, it may be more difficult these days than ever before."*

A recent John Glenn graduate, Craig Donley, told the students that he had tried to kill himself after years of abusing drugs. Addicted to cocaine and other drugs, he had dropped to 155 out of 160 in the class ranking. "I didn't care about anything except drugs," said Donley. "I tried to quit and would last two days . . . and then I decided to take the easy way out."

He took nearly an entire bottle of sleeping pills and downed it with kitchen ammonia. When he woke up, he was in a hospital. "My family was there. It was Christmas Day, and I suddenly realized how much they cared."

Donley enrolled in a detox program and received special permission to return to school, with Pantaleno's encouragement. "I went back to school, and people couldn't believe it," Donley said. "I started doing all my work. I got straight A's." Donley graduated as John Glenn's "most improved student" last spring. Now 18 he is an engaging, clean-cut student at Suffolk Community College— virtually unrecognizable from the shaggy, drug-addicted teenager who once roamed the school hallways of John Glenn avoiding eye contact.

Substance abuse is involved in many suicide attempts, a fact educators tried to pound into the teens. "The reality is that life is painful," said Frank Monastero, a social worker from the Hospice of the South Shore. "The only way to get through the pain is to confront it. Not sedate it."

Observed 14-year-old Tami Altschuler: "People who try to commit suicide think, 'When I'm gone, then they will be sorry.' But that's not fair to yourself."

That is one of the key lessons that an array of recent programs like John Glenn's is trying to get across. Port Washington High School, for instance, has started a suicide hot line. Brentwood's Freshman Center has targeted 150 of its 900 students for intervention by a team of teachers and professionals. Others focus on "peer counseling" as a way to ease students toward professional help. By encouraging students to share with each other, often by taking oaths of confidentiality, schools are finding that teenagers often find comfort. Many schools participate in a program called Natural Helpers, where a group of students is nominated by classmates to serve as peer counselors. Those selected attend a three-day retreat away from school to learn how to help fellow students with problems.

"The reality is young people are coming into contact with a lot of serious issues we didn't deal with until we were much older," said Tom Schiel, a school psychologist at Levittown's Division Avenue High School, which offers such a peer counseling program. "We're seeing young people dealing with sophisticated problems before they are emotionally able."

Pantaleno and other North Shore psychologists have written a platform paper asking schools to pay more attention to the emotional needs of students. "We feel that we are pedaling as fast as we can and that we're still losing," Pantaleno said. Eighty of John Glenn's 600 students signed up for "Awareness Weekend," but Pantaleno was sure he was missing some who could have used it.

After the lights went on at the close of Friday night's "sharing session," a group of girls clustered around a *Seventeen* magazine, amazed and somewhat gratified that they had seen some normally stoic boys shed some tears. Kids flooded into the gym, which was kept open for all-night volleyball, basketball and Ping-Pong games. Kevin Greene, one of the school's peer helpers, set up his band, U-Turn, for a late-night concert, which filled the auditorium when the first guitar strums echoed through the empty halls. Others watched the women's Olympic figure-skating championships, wondering aloud how the young skaters could keep their poise at their age.

No one got more than two hours' sleep—in separate rooms for girls and boys monitored by adults—before the lights went on Saturday morning at 7. Most of the teenagers were still half asleep when the first session of the day started, a talk about death and bereavement.

> *"By encouraging students to share with each other, often by taking oaths of confidentiality, schools are finding that teenagers often find comfort."*

But during the night they were locked in school, something important had begun to happen. Kids who had never spoken to each other started to hang out. And they seemed to find solace in each other's problems and hope that things would get better.

"One of the basic objectives of the weekend was to break down cliques," said Janna Newton, 16, who said she had been surprised at how many of her peers were willing to share painful problems. "I think it worked."

"It's just so important to talk," added Tom Scarola, 14.

Three days later, after classes had resumed again, freshman Ellen Dano, 14, wrote a poem about what the weekend had meant to her. She called it "My Time of Liberation." It concluded:

Each day a coat of paint set on my mask dwindles
  as I probe myself and stand up for myself.
Only then does my time of liberation take place.
Only then am I saved.

Gun Control Would Help Prevent Suicide

by The Educational Fund to End Handgun Violence and The Coalition to Stop Gun Violence

About the authors: *The Educational Fund to End Handgun Violence is a non-profit organization that seeks to reduce gun violence through the legal system, educational services, and support of grassroots activists. The Coalition to Stop Gun Violence is a research and advocacy organization that seeks to control the sale and manufacture of guns and reduce gun-related violence.*

Every year, firearm suicides account for just less than half of all firearm deaths and yet both sides of the gun control debate, along with the media and the general public, have shied away from this topic. It is time for the American people to understand that in looking for solutions to crime and violence by keeping a handgun at home they are placing themselves, and young people who often act impulsively, at much greater risk. More than 17,000 Americans die annually from self-inflicted firearm injuries. This staggering death toll would be greatly reduced if handguns were removed from homes.

Although firearm murders occupy the media spotlight, in reality, guns are used most frequently for self-destructive purposes. One study revealed that "[f]irearm suicides outnumbered firearm homicides in 40 of the 50 years between 1933 and 1982." In 1992 (the last year for which statistics are available) 37,776 Americans died as a result of firearm injuries. Of these firearm-related deaths, 18,169 (or 48 percent) were suicides, while 17,790 (or 47 percent) were homicides. The remaining firearm deaths were caused by unintentional shootings.

In 1992, suicide was the ninth leading cause of death in the United States, accounting for the loss of 30,484 lives. Almost 60 percent of these suicides were completed with guns. The same year 3,073 youths nationwide between 15- and 24-years-old killed themselves with a gun.

Statistics illustrate the extent of the problem of suicide in the United States. Nevertheless, the data are potentially misleading underestimates of actual fig-

Excerpted with permission from *The Unspoken Tragedy: Firearm Suicide in the United States,* by The Educational Fund to End Handgun Violence and The Coalition to Stop Gun Violence, May 31, 1995.

ures due to under-reporting. One national team of researchers estimates that deaths resulting from suicide are attributed to other causes as much as 25–50 percent of the time.

In the United States, white males, Native Americans, and the elderly experience the highest rates of suicide. During the past four decades, however, rates among groups traditionally considered at low-risk of committing suicide increased dramatically. Firearm suicides account for most, if not all, of this growth.

Firearms as a Method of Suicide

Firearms are the most common means of suicide in the United States for both genders and all age groups. Scientific studies reach varying conclusions regarding the use of handguns versus long guns in firearm suicides. It is often assumed that long guns are less likely than handguns to be used for suicide. However, David A. Brent et al. reports that for his study sample the presence of rifles and shotguns presented as great a suicide risk as the presence of handguns. The researchers found that any gun in the home increases the risk of suicide. Suicidal adolescents are 75 times more likely to commit suicide when a gun is kept in their home.

Research indicates the suicide method that is most available and socially acceptable will be employed most often. In the United States, firearms meet both criteria. Thus, it is no surprise that guns are the most prevalent means of suicide. A study comparing the regional rates of firearm prevalence and suicide found a 3.0 per 100,000 persons increase in the suicide rate per 10% increase in the household prevalence of firearms. If we hope to reduce the number of suicides committed in the United States we must simultaneously decrease or at least stabilize the number of guns in circulation and weaken the social conception that firearms pose little or no danger to owners and their families. . . .

Suicide Attempts Versus Completions

Mark L. Rosenberg et al. maintains "nonfatal assaults and suicide attempts may outnumber homicides and suicides by a ratio of more than 100 to 1." O'Carroll et al. estimates "that there are approximately 25 suicide attempts for every completed suicide and that there are 750,000 adults who attempt suicide each year." A study of fatal and nonfatal suicide attempts by adolescents in Oregon from 1988–1993 reported 31 nonfatal adolescent suicide attempts for every suicide fatality. The study also revealed 75.5% of reported suicide attempts used drugs as the method of suicide. Yet, drug-related suicides represented 0.4% of the suicide fatalities. In comparison, firearm-related suicides accounted for 0.6% of total suicide attempts, but 78.2% of the suicide fatalities.

The use of firearms has a high correlation to fatality. One study of suicide attempts and fatalities reported that 69% of the study sample died as a result of a firearm suicide. Whereas, none of the surviving suicide victims used a gun in their attempt.

Historically, males have completed suicide two to five times more often than females. Researchers maintain the historic discrepancy between male and female suicide fatality rates results from differences in choice of method. Males in fact attempt suicide much less often than females, but use highly lethal methods, such as inflicting firearm injuries or hanging, when they do. From 1988–1991, 65 percent of male suicide deaths resulted from firearms. Females, on the other hand, attempt suicide an estimated two to nine times more frequently, but employ

> *"Firearms are the most common means of suicide in the United States for both genders and all age groups."*

less lethal means, such as poisoning, that provide windows of opportunity for rescue and medical treatment. Nevertheless, firearms are today the most common method used in female suicide fatalities.

Given the prevalence of suicide attempts compared to suicide completions it is evident that the lethality of the method involved is of critical importance. If the estimated 750,000 individuals attempting suicide each year were to do so with firearms, the national rate of suicide death would skyrocket. Not only are guns deadly because of their high degree of lethality in suicide attempts, but their increasing prevalence causes more suicide attempts. One study predicts that if handgun prevalence were to reach 100 percent in the United States, the suicide rate would reach 42.6 per 100,000 (compared to the 1992 rate of 12.0 per 100,000). In the interest of preventing such large numbers from ending their lives it is necessary to ensure that firearm access does not exceed its current rate.

The Theory of Method Substitution

It has been proposed that suicidal individuals will find ways to kill themselves regardless of the availability of means. According to this hypothesis, if someone who wanted to die did not have access to a gun he or she would seek another method rather than abandoning his or her plans.

Several scientific studies have explored the issue of method substitution in suicide. One study investigated the cooking and heating gas in Birmingham, England, which once contained high levels of carbon monoxide and frequently was employed in suicide attempts. Between 1963 and 1970 this poisonous element was removed from the gas. Afterward, there was "a dramatic reduction in both unintentional and suicidal fatal carbon monoxide poisoning. Suicide incidence by other methods stayed almost the same. In other words, a common lethal agent was removed and use of others did not take its place."

Another study investigated the impact of gun regulations on homicide and suicide rates in Washington, DC. In 1976, Washington, DC, implemented a law prohibiting local residents from buying or selling handguns. Loftin found the regulation "was associated with a prompt decline in homicides and suicides by firearms in the District of Columbia. No such decline was observed for homicides or suicides in which guns were not used, and no decline was seen in adjacent metropolitan areas where restrictive licensing did not apply."

Brent et al. maintains that youths would be less likely to substitute an alternative suicide method if guns were not easily accessed:

> [M]ethod substitution may be less likely to occur in adolescents and young adults, possibly because of the prominent role that impulsivity and substance abuse play in youthful suicide. The availability of a gun may play a more critical role in determining the lethality of a suicide attempt among impulsive youth than in older adults for whom suicide is a more premeditated act. . . .

Research on suicide method substitution remains inconclusive. However, it is possible that some suicide attempts may not occur if the means were difficult to obtain. Regardless, the argument that suicidal individuals would substitute an alternative means for killing themselves if a gun were not available ultimately becomes moot when one considers the lethality of the method. The vast majority of firearm suicide attempts result in immediate fatalities. Suicide attempts by other means, such as ingestion of poison or exposure to high quantities of carbon monoxide, allow time for a change of heart and/or medical intervention. Thus, a decrease in availability of guns would save lives. . . .

Historical Trends

The national rate of suicide for all ages in aggregate rose somewhat steadily from a low point of approximately 10 per 100,000 in 1943 to a high point of 13 per 100,000 in 1986. Since then, the rate has leveled off. In 1992, the national rate for all ages combined was 12.0. Susan P. Baker et al. reports that between 1968 and 1986, the firearm suicide rate "increased by 36 percent, while suicide by all other means combined remained virtually unchanged."

In the past, the overwhelming majority of suicide victims in the United States were older white males. During the last few decades, however, suicide rates have increased among new demographic groups including females and adolescents:

> Although the rate of suicide remains highest among older white males, rates of suicide have grown disproportionately in groups that were traditionally at low risk, and increasing rates of firearm suicide appear to be a striking part of this dynamic transformation. Between 1960 and 1980 the total number of females committing suicide by all means other than firearms increased 16 percent, while the number of females committing suicide using firearms more than doubled. Suicide of young persons ages 5–19 by all means other than firearms increased 175 percent between 1960 and 1980; over the same period the percentage increase of suicide by firearms among this age group was 299 percent. Nonwhites, typically a low-risk group for suicide, experienced an 88 percent increase in non-firearm suicides between 1960 and 1980, compared with a 160 percent increase in the volume of firearm suicide. . . .

A lack of data precludes drawing a causal link between an increase in gun availability and an increase in firearm suicide rates. Nevertheless, research reveals the two trends clearly are associated.

In the 1960s and 1970s the number of firearms circulating throughout the United States sky-rocketed with the tripling of firearm imports and domestic production during this period. The Bureau of Alcohol, Tobacco and Firearms released a report that estimated 54 million firearms in circulation in the United States in 1950; 104 million in 1970; and over 200 million in 1989. From 1989 to 1995, domestic producers have poured out approximately 3.5 million guns annually, while importers have contributed another half million each year. Researchers estimate that in 1968 there were 50 guns per 100 civilians. In contrast, by 1979, there were approximately 75 guns per 100 civilians. Numerous polls indicate about 50% of Americans admit to having a gun at home. Today there are approximately 220 million guns in the U.S., which equals all the adults and more than half the children in America.

This noteworthy increase in firearm ownership corresponds to a drastic jump in firearm suicide rates. Whereas firearms were responsible for 47 percent of all suicides in 1960, they were responsible for 56 percent of all suicides by 1977 and 61 percent by 1990. One researcher noted that "[v]irtually all of the increase [in suicide rates] since 1963 has been in suicide by firearms."

Youth Suicide Rates

In the United States the highest suicide rates occur among the elderly. While the nation's overall suicide rate appears to have reached a plateau, youth suicide rates continue to climb, marking a distinct and alarming shift in suicides to the youngest age groups. Youths also have experienced a rise in firearm suicide rates greater than any other age group in the country.

Prior to 1955 the suicide rate for youths aged 15- to 24-years in the United States remained constant at a much lower point than the national rate for all ages combined. Starting in the mid-1950s, however, the suicide rate among this age group began to increase significantly. In 1950, the suicide rate for persons 15- to 24-years of age was 4.5 per 100,000. By 1980, the suicide rate for the same age group had increased more than 300 percent to over 12.0 per 100,000.

> *"If the estimated 750,000 individuals attempting suicide each year were to do so with firearms, the national rate of suicide death would skyrocket."*

In 1992, the suicide rate for 15- to 19-year-olds was still higher at 13.0 per 100,000, and exceeded the national rate for all ages combined of 12.0 per 100,000.

In an effort to address the escalating problem of youth suicide, the US Department of Health and Human Services in 1979 set a public health goal to lower the suicide rate for 15- to 24-year-olds from the 1978 rate of 12.4 per 100,000 to less than 11.0 per 100,000 by 1990. In 1992, however, this goal still had not been reached, and the suicide rate for this age group in fact had worsened further.

The self-destructive use of guns is the most common method of suicide for young people in the United States. Guns are largely, if not entirely, responsible for the dramatic increase in suicide rates for the nation's youths. Since 1970, firearm suicide has risen three times more quickly than suicide by other means among 15- to 19-year-olds, and ten times more quickly among 20- to 24-year-olds. During the years 1980–1992, the suicide rate for persons 15- to 19-years of age increased 28.3%, of which firearm-related suicides account for 81%. Today, approximately 60 percent of all teenagers in the United States who complete a suicide do so with guns.

Data indicate that even younger children are falling victim to the same phenomenon. Both the firearm-related and the overall suicide rate has increased for 10- to 14-year-olds in the United States. For the years 1980–1992, the suicide rate for young people aged 10 to 14 increased 120% overall. Firearms are now the most frequent method of suicide for males as well as females within this age group.

Youth Exposure to Firearms

Youths in the United States today have greater exposure and access to guns. A survey conducted by the Harvard School of Public Health in 1993 reported startling findings regarding the ease with which youths today can obtain guns:

> A substantial 59–21 percent majority of all young people aged 10–19 in school today say they "could get a handgun if I wanted one." In the central cities 63 percent say they could get one, as do 58 percent of those in the suburbs, and 56 percent in small towns and rural areas.

> Two in three who know where to get a handgun say they could get one within a 24 hour period. A higher proportion of young people who go to private and parochial schools say they know how to get a gun than do those who go to public schools.

Nationally, one out of two households admits to possessing firearms. In homes where there is both a child and a gun, odds are the gun is stored dangerously—accessible and loaded. Among parents who admit to having a gun in their home, 59% also admit that their firearm is not locked away from their children.

It is possible that the gun culture surrounding youths contributes to the rampant increase in youth firearm suicide in recent decades. As youths gain greater access in our increasingly gun-saturated society, it is more likely that they will employ a gun as a means of suicide.

The Role of Impulse in Youth Suicide

The decision to end one's life is frequently sudden, uncalculated, and fleeting. It is that much more so for adolescents. Firearms are one of the most lethal means of suicide available. Easy access to highly lethal methods significantly increases the likelihood of an impulsive suicide attempt resulting in death. Whereas other methods, such as drug overdoses, allow time for medical intervention, firearms usually produce instant fatalities. Nevertheless, firearms are widely prevalent in homes throughout the United States. Consequently, young people—a group particularly prone to impulsive acts—often have little difficulty locating a gun at home, leading to a lethal suicide attempt that was far from premeditated or sincere.

"Easy access to highly lethal methods significantly increases the likelihood of an impulsive suicide attempt resulting in death."

Researchers have determined that youths who attempt suicide rarely have a "clear and sustained" desire to die. One study of adolescent attempters found two-thirds did not in fact have any desire to die. Instead, youth suicide attempts frequently constitute highly impulsive efforts to communicate strong emotions or a cry for help. Access to firearms under such circumstances is very problematic as guns are associated with such a high degree of lethality providing little opportunity for second thoughts or outside intervention. . . .

We propose a two-pronged approach to the problem of firearm suicide. We must reduce both the demand and the supply of guns in this country.

Public education campaigns must inform the public about the dangers of firearm ownership. We must reveal the fallacy of "protecting" one's family with a gun in the home. People must learn that a gun in the home puts themselves and their family at risk. We also must de-glamorize guns and offer youth opportunities to make positive contributions to their community.

Regulation of firearms and enforcement of existing laws must be increased in order to cap, if not reduce, the number of guns in circulation and thereby decrease access to one of the most lethal methods of suicide. Most importantly, individuals must acknowledge the risks associated with firearm ownership and remove and/or ban guns from their homes.

Gun Control Would Not Prevent Suicide

by Don B. Kates et al.

About the author: *Don B. Kates is a civil rights lawyer based in San Francisco, California, where he also teaches and writes on criminology-related issues.*

Predictably, gun violence, particularly homicide, is a major study topic for social scientists, particularly criminologists. Less predictably, gun crime, accidents, and suicide are also a topic of study among medical and public health professionals. Our focus is the remarkable difference between the way medical and public health writers, on the one hand, and social scientists, on the other, treat firearms issues. . . .

The health advocate shibboleth [belief] posits a simple, simplistic, pattern: More guns means more homicide, suicide, and fatal gun accidents; stricter gun control means fewer such tragedies. As we shall see, this is contradicted by the trend in fatal gun accidents. In 1967, for instance, 2,896 Americans died in gun accidents; but, because the vast increase in guns over the next twenty years was accompanied by a steady decline in such fatalities, in 1986 there were only 1,452 fatal gun accidents. The health sages deal with this by simply not mentioning it in relation to their shibboleth; indeed, they generally avoid mentioning the dramatic downward trend in accidental fatalities at all using instead a figure for fatal accidents in some particular year or the combined figure for fatal accidents over a series of years so as to obscure the actual trend.

Misuse of Statistics

Similar statistical legerdemain [sleighting of hand] is required to counterfeit a case for their shibboleth vis-à-vis suicide and murder. We discuss below its refutation by the decline in homicide which accompanied the increasing gun ownership during the early and mid-1980s. To mask the embarrassing downward trend in murder, the health sages began "massaging" the statistics by combining homicide and suicide in one joint figure. This produced an "Intentional Homicide" rate which, once again, they claimed was caused by widespread gun ownership.

But this approach leads to another embarrassing outcome: Though the U.S. has more suicide than homicide, Europe and many other areas have higher yet suicide rates. Consider what would happen to the homicide rate-only international comparison made, strangely enough, by Professor Susan Baker, who originated the combined homicide-suicide approach to American statistics. Lauding Denmark's strict gun laws, she emphasizes that Denmark's murder rate is lower than America's by about seven deaths per one hundred thousand population. But making the same comparison as to suicide would show the Danish rate to be much higher than the American. If we combine the suicide and murder figures according to Baker's own (supposedly preferable) method, the Danish death rate per one hundred thousand population is almost 50 percent higher than the American!

"The lowest [suicide] rate is for Israel, a country that actually encourages widespread gun possession."

Combining suicide and murder statistics in comparing the U.S. to other countries would not serve the health advocates' political agenda. So, it is only when they discuss U.S. figures that Baker and the other health sages combine murder and suicide figures. In making foreign comparisons they continue to separate out the American murder rate and use it only. . . . Of eighteen nations for which figures were readily available, the U.S. ranks below the median when suicide and homicide rates are combined; the U.S. combined homicide/suicide rate is less than half the combined murder/suicide rate in Hungary (where guns were very severely controlled until the fall of Communism) and less than one-third the suicide rate alone of gun-banning Rumania; such relatively firearm-intensive countries as Australia and New Zealand rank low on the table; and the lowest rate is for Israel, a country that actually encourages widespread gun possession.

Reviewing the entire health advocacy literature on guns and suicide, we have been unable to find even one reference to the much greater suicide rates in antigun European countries. A *fortiori* that literature never discusses is why antigun nations have so much more suicide if the more-guns-means-more-suicide shibboleth is correct. Sloan et al. followed their ludicrous Seattle-Vancouver homicide comparison with an (unintentionally) hilarious comparison of suicide rates in those two cities. Completely unfazed by the fact that Vancouver had the higher suicide rate, Sloan et al. emphasize that it had a lower suicide rate for one subgroup, adolescents and young men. This, they solemnly intone, is due to the U.S. having lax gun laws and more gun availability.

Suicide Among Young Males

This brings us to an issue health advocacy articles stressed during the 1980s: the poignant phenomenon of suicide among young males, which was supposed to be increasing because of growing firearm availability. Naturally, no health advocate mentioned that suicide among teenagers and young adults has been increasing in much of the industrialized world. By the same token, readers of health advocacy articles blaming American suicide increases in these groups on guns will never learn: (a) that while suicide among American males aged 15–24 increased 7.4 percent in the period 1980–90, (b) the increase in England for this group was over ten times greater (78 percent), with car exhaust poisoning being used most often.

Despite recent increases in youth suicide, the population subgroup most likely to shoot themselves are elderly men. We take leave to doubt that any health advocate (or anyone else) is wise enough to decide for a 76-year-old man in failing health whether he should live or die. But such philosophical considerations are never mentioned by health sages asserting the more-guns-mean-more-suicide shibboleth—nor is modesty about their own wisdom likely to find favor with sages who are confident enough of it to be willing to promote their policy prescription for American society through a literature of deceit.

Setting aside the philosophical issue, it is pragmatically arguable that, if guns are unavailable, people who are seriously enough interested in killing themselves will find some other way. On the other hand, some suicides may occur impulsively because of the immediate availability of a deadly mechanism to a person who might not have completed the act had time for reflection been required. The intellectual desert inhabited by antigun health advocates is epitomized by their failure (or inability) to cite the strongest empirical showing for gun control as a means of reducing suicide. They do not know of this study because it was done by Gary Kleck, whose work they compulsively avoid. Suicide is a serious issue deserving of serious scholarly discussion, rather than use as a political football by unscrupulous propagandists grasping at any opportunity to make a case for their preordained agenda.

> *"[Health advocacy] literature never discusses why antigun nations have so much more suicide if the more-guns-means-more-suicide shibboleth is correct."*

Suicide Should Not Be Prevented

by Thomas Szasz

About the author: *Thomas Szasz is the author of numerous books on psychiatry, including* The Myth of Mental Illness *and* A Lexicon of Lunacy.

My aim in this viewpoint is to rebut the contemporary view that suicide is a mental health problem, that psychiatric practitioners and institutions have a professional duty to try to prevent it, and that it is a legitimate function of the state to empower such professionals and institutions—especially psychiatrists and mental hospitals—to impose coercive interventions on persons diagnosed as posing a suicidal risk. Because of these assumptions, should a person formally identified as a patient kill himself while in the care of a mental health clinician or clinic, the latter is likely to be sued for, and may be found guilty of, professional negligence for failing to prevent his suicide.

I reject this perspective and offer, instead, another view of suicide—as that of an act by a moral agent, for which that agent himself is ultimately responsible. Rejecting suicide prevention in principle, and eschewing it as a professional practice, would protect the mental health clinician from having to play self-contradictory roles; would protect the mental health client from having to submit to coercion in the name of suicide prevention; and would protect the American people from having to pay for a so-called health policy that undermines the ethic of self-responsibility on which our nation ostensibly rests.

Prevention Implies Coercion

I want to emphasize, at the outset, that I am opposed only to coercive methods of preventing, or trying to prevent, suicide. However, it would be mendacious to deny that, in practice, suicide prevention rests on the use of force, or on the threat of its use, to restrain the would-be suicide. Indeed, the term *prevention,* bracketed with the term *suicide,* implies coercion. Preventive medical measures, exemplified by vaccinating children against contagious diseases, are typically (although not always) backed by the force of the law. In contrast, advice, guidance, or instruction regarding pregnancy or marriage are called abortion and marriage "counseling." It would be awkward, and wrong, to call such counseling "abortion prevention," "marriage prevention," or "divorce prevention."

Psychiatrists (and other mental health professionals) bear an especially heavy burden of responsibility with respect to the moral dilemmas posed by suicide; hence, they must be especially thoughtful and forthright about where they come down on the issue of coercive suicide prevention. Just as mental health professionals reject—as ethically and professionally unacceptable—sexual relations between therapists and clients, so they could also reject—as ethically and professionally unacceptable—coercing clients who they think or fear might kill themselves. Alternatively, mental health professionals could individually choose to accept or reject coercive suicide prevention as a part of the service they render—each practitioner clearly identified to the public by his stance toward this practice. Anyone identified as a therapist or member of a helping profession could thus elect to embrace coercive suicide prevention, as the psychiatrist—qua lifesaving clinician in the hospital—typically does, and is expected to do by custom and law; or he could eschew such coercion, as the priest—qua soul-saving cleric in the confessional—does, and is required to do by custom, religion, and law. Opting for either course would be defensible and moral. But, given the dilemmas posed by suicide and suicide prevention, trying to play both roles at once and claiming to serve the best interests of both the individual and society, is impossible to achieve and immoral to attempt.

> *"[Suicide is] an act by a moral agent, for which that agent himself is ultimately responsible."*

Failure to prevent suicide is now one of the leading reasons for successful malpractice suits against psychiatrists and psychiatric institutions. This situation is the inevitable consequence of the way suicide is now viewed by mental health professionals, lawyers, judges, and other educated persons. . . .

The Image of Suicide

The psychiatrically popularized image of suicide today—as a mental abnormality or illness, or a symptom of such a condition—explains why mental health professionals, philosophers, and ethicists, as well as lay persons, are all so skittish about suicide that it is virtually impossible to engage in a reasoned examination of this subject. Why is suicide considered to be a priori bad or undesirable? And, if it is considered bad because it injures society, then why is it not treated as a crime, as it used to be, and punished by the state? Or, if it is considered bad because it injures the victim's soul, then why is it not treated as a sin, as it used to be, and punished by the Church? (Persons who kill themselves are no longer denied a Christian or Jewish burial.) Finally, if suicide is considered bad because it injures both the suicide and others, like a disease (as people now seem to believe), then why is it not treated by specialists who know how to treat "it"? But who knows how to "treat" suicide? No one.

Instead of seriously pondering such questions, people now prefer to explain away the problem of suicide by claiming to view it scientifically, creating an image of it that combines the features not only of sin, sickness, and crime, but also of irrationality, incompetence, and insanity. The result is a stubborn unwillingness to view suicide as we view other morally freighted acts—like abortion or divorce—as good or bad, desirable or undesirable, depending on the circumstances in which the act occurs and the criteria by which it is judged. . . .

Why do psychiatrists (and other mental health professionals) seek and receive special privileges and powers to intervene in the lives of so-called suicidal persons? Because in the modern view, the person who threatens to commit suicide or actually does so is typically considered to be mentally ill. I need not belabor the contention that this is an absurd, parochial view of what may well be life's oldest existential option and greatest moral challenge. There is, of course, not a shred of historical, philosophical, or medical support for viewing suicide as different, in principle, from other acts or important decisions, such as getting married or divorced or having a child.

The phrase *suicide prevention* is itself a misleading slogan characteristic of our therapeutic age. Insofar as suicide is a physical possibility, there can be no suicide prevention. Insofar as suicide is a fundamental right, there ought to be no coercive suicide

> *"Claiming to serve the best interests of both the individual and society is impossible to achieve and immoral to attempt."*

prevention measures or programs. If one person is to prevent another person from killing himself, the former obviously cannot, and should not be expected to, accomplish that task unless he can exercise complete control over the suicidal person. But it is either impossible to do this, or would require reducing the subject to a social status beneath that of a slave. The slave is compelled only to labor against his will; whereas the person forcibly prevented from killing himself is compelled to live against his will.

None of this means that an individual troubled by suicidal ideas or impulses should be denied the assistance he seeks, provided he can find others willing to render such assistance. It means only that expressions of so-called suicidal behavior—in any of their now-familiar psychopathological forms or shapes, such as suicidal ideation, suicidal impulse, suicide attempt, and so forth—would no longer qualify as a justification for coercing the subject. Were such a policy adopted, people would have to make do with noncoercive methods of preventing suicide, just as they must now make do with noncoercive methods of preventing other forms of self-harming actions, such as warnings on packages of cigarettes or on bottles of beer.

No one can deny that policies aimed at preventing suicide by means of legal and psychiatric coercion imply a paternalistic attitude toward the patient, and require giving certain privileges and powers to a special class of protectors vis-à-vis a special class of victims. All such solutions for human problems are purchased at the cost of creating the classic problem of "Who shall guard the guardians?" The demonstrable harms generated by the mistakes and misuses of the powers of mental health professionals and judges (delegated to them on the ground that they are protecting suicidal persons from themselves) must be balanced against the alleged or ostensible benefits generated by coercive policies of suicide prevention. Since we have no generally agreed upon criteria for adjudicating controversies concerning such a trade-off, our acceptance or rejection of coercive suicide prevention is best viewed as a manifestation of our moral principles and psychiatric premises—especially about free will and personal responsibility on the one hand, and mental illness and therapeutic paternalism on the other hand. . . .

In short, I object to our present policies of suicide prevention because they downgrade the responsibility of the individual (called a "patient," even if he explicitly rejects that role) for the conduct of his own life and death. Because I value individual liberty highly and am convinced that liberty and responsibility are indivisible, I want to enlarge the scope of liberty and responsibility. In the present instance, this means opposing policies of suicide prevention that minimize the responsibility of individuals for killing themselves, and supporting policies that maximize their responsibility for doing so. . . .

Such reflections incline me to believe that it would be morally and politically desirable to accord suicide the status of a basic human right (in its strict, political-philosophical sense). When I say this, I emphatically do not mean that killing oneself is, ipso facto, good or praiseworthy (a disclaimer I emphasize only because the meaning of the word *right* is now often so misinterpreted). I mean only that the power of the state should not be legitimately deployed to prohibit or prevent persons from killing themselves. The point is simple but often forgotten: For example, when we say that freedom of religion is a right, we do not mean that we must accept all religions as equally ethical or fit for modern life; we mean only that we ought to abstain from deploying the power of the state to promote the religion we like, and prohibit those we dislike.

> *"People now prefer to explain away the problem of suicide by claiming to view it scientifically."*

Actually, the distinction between the illegal and the immoral is deeply ingrained in Anglo-American law. Thus, certain acts are regarded not only as crimes but also as violations of widely shared moral values: for example, the unprovoked killing of another person is a *malum in se,* a wrong in itself. Certain other acts are regarded as crimes only because they violate existing laws without being immoral: for example, a parking violation is a *malum prohibitum,* a wrong because it is prohibited. Finally, there are acts some people regard as wrongs to be prohibited by law, but others do not: for example, Jim Crow laws or drug laws. In a free, secular society, such prohibitions ought to be illegal, because the behaviors they seek to control deprive no one of life, liberty, or property; they merely offend the values of a particular caste or creed.

"In the modern view, the person who threatens to commit suicide or actually does so is typically considered to be mentally ill."

The effort to seriously ponder the issue of suicide probes some of our most passionately held, but not universally shared, beliefs about ending our own lives. Is killing oneself like homicide, and hence properly called "suicide?" Or is it more like birth control, and better termed "death control"? As polls and other evidence clearly show, Americans view suicide ambivalently, as both a dreaded enemy and a trusted friend.

The belief that it is the legitimate function of the state to coerce persons because they might kill themselves is a characteristically modern, quasi-therapeutic idea, catering at once to our craving for dependency and omnipotence. The result is an intricate web of interventions and institutions that have themselves become powerful engines of hypocrisy and seemingly indispensable mechanisms for satisfying human needs now buried in hidden agendas.

It has taken a long time to get mental health professionals deeply enmeshed in the suicide business, and it will take a long time to get them out of it. In the meantime, mental health professionals and their clients are doomed to wander aimlessly in the existential-legal labyrinth generated by treating suicide as if it constituted a mental health problem. However, if we refuse to play a part in the drama of coercive suicide prevention, then we shall be sorely tempted to conclude that mental health professionals and their partners in suicide richly deserve each other and the torment each is so ready and eager to inflict on the other.

Suicide Should Be Prevented

by Andrew E. Slaby

About the author: *Andrew E. Slaby is a clinical professor of psychiatry at New York University and New York Medical College.*

Evaluating and managing suicidal outpatients has long made clinicians fearful. Now, as managed and capitated care continues limiting hospitalizations and outpatient treatments, clinicians have become even more anxious about treating patients who are suicidal. Fortunately, a few basic principles of patient management greatly facilitate treating self-destructive outpatients and preventing their suicides.

It is not always possible to prevent suicide, but in most instances the impulse can be significantly reduced when clinicians, patients and patients' families understand the factors that impact suicide risk. Hopelessness, more than depression, predicts suicide. Patients who suicide do not want to die; they simply want to end their pain. When they can see another way to end the pain, they use it. People kill themselves when they feel there is no alternate way to ameliorate their anguish. Many of these deaths could be avoided if these individuals had received aggressive treatment, psychopharmacological therapy, and had their social supports rallied to assist them.

The majority of suicides had psychiatric diagnoses that, if identified and treated, would have diminished the risk of suicide. When initially seen, all patients should be asked if they have ever considered suicide, if they are currently suicidal, and if they have ever made an attempt. Developing a plan for managing suicidal impulses begins with the therapist's first encounter with the patient, or arises during the course of treatment when patients fail to respond to diagnostic-specific treatments.

Characteristics of Suicidal People

Risk Assessment   Approximately 60 percent of all suicides suffer major depression, and 15 percent of the patients with major depression die by suicide.

Twenty percent of the people who suicide suffer disorders with a strong affective component, such as a dysthymic disorder [a form of depression], post-traumatic stress disorder, or schizoaffective disorder. Of the remaining 20 percent who die, a few are so-called "rational" suicides. It is notable that over 10 percent of those stating they want to suicide because they have an incurable illness do not have the illness; instead they have a monosymptomatic delusional disorder with the false belief that they have a fatal illness.

Study after study confirms that most individuals who commit suicide suffer from depression. Such affectively ill patients, as a group, are especially creative as artists, politicians, and entrepreneurs; their loss to suicide represents not only a loss of life but society's disproportional loss of their talents. Individuals who are gay—especially adolescents—or who have anxiety disorders or learning disorders are at increased risk. An unrecognized learning disorder such as attention deficit hyperactivity disorder (ADHD) can lead to poor school performance despite superior intelligence. A child whose best efforts fail first becomes demoralized, and then falls hopeless as teachers and family fail to recognize the disorder. Some young people self-medicate ADHD or depression with recreational stimulants (e.g., speed or cocaine) or alcohol, further enhancing their impulsivity and risk.

> *"Most suicides are preventable."*

Hospitalization   Most individuals with suicidal thoughts do not require hospitalization; only when their desire to die or impulsivity is great is this necessary. Their suicide risk is greatest shortly after a recent suicide attempt, especially if they have a plan to try again if no relief is forthcoming. Hopelessness, psychosis, absence of social supports, substance abuse, and impulsivity all indicate an increased need for observation and sometimes restraint in a protected environment. Extremely suicidal patients, even in a hospital, may require "arms length" observation to prevent self-harm.

Drugs and Other Therapy

Psychopharmacotherapy   In most instances, appropriate psychopharmacotherapy remarkably reduces suicide risk. If the immediate risk of impulsive suicide is exceptionally great, or if symptoms fail to respond to medication, electroshock therapy may be needed.

Most suicides result from fundamental changes in neurotransmitters in the brain that impair perception and affect, resulting in a sense of hopelessness and impulsivity leading to attempts that end in death. The neurochemical defect appears in most cases to be a deficiency of serotonin reflected in a decrease in its principle metabolite, 5-hydroxyindole acetic acid, in the cerebrospinal fluid. This decrease is associated not only with suicide but also homicide. Regardless of their diagnosis, individuals with decreased brain serotonin are also at risk for homicide and for severe and impulsive suicide attempts.

A new generation of antidepressants—the selective serotonin reuptake inhibitors (SSRIs)—specifically remedy serotonin deficiency, improving impulsivity, depression, eating disorders and obsessive compulsive disorders, and reducing symptoms of other disorders which increase suicide risk. The wide safety margin of these SSRIs reduces the hazards of overdose seen with older antidepressant drugs.

Who Is at Risk?

Social Support People at greatest risk for suicide are the most socially isolated: particularly divorced, single, or separated men in late life. As adolescents, gay youth do not have support for their gender identity, resulting in their over-representation among adolescent suicides. Support groups for HIV-positive patients, gay youths, and single parents reduce some stress by reducing isolation and allowing sharing of coping skills.

Psychoeducation Patients, families, clergy, caregivers, and others should be taught to recognize individuals at risk, and they should be educated to the role of medication, therapy, and social support in reducing suicide risk. Weight loss, social isolation, sleep disturbances, impulsivity, decreasing work and school performance, and agitation indicate worsening depression. Lack of plans for the future and giving away of prized possessions suggest an evolving plan to die.

Access to Help All patients at risk should be provided with the therapists' phone numbers, their backups, and places to call if neither respond in a timely manner. Lack of access to help at a time of despair may result in panic, anger and impulsive acts.

Realistic Goals The anxiety of caregivers and family members is reduced by mutual understanding of the limits to what is possible. Most depressions respond to antidepressants—many with the first drug chosen—but side effects can limit choice and dosage. The suicide risk may increase in therapy when patients' energy returns before their feelings of hopelessness, helplessness, and worthlessness abate. Schizophrenia, on the other hand, has the same lifetime risk of suicide as major depression, but a somewhat worse prognosis. What works at one point in the course of treatment may not be effective at another point, and management of the illness needs to be altered as circumstances dictate. In some instances, a long time is required for diminution of the desire to die. Even more time may be required to restore or acquire a lust for life that, in itself, would counter a desire to die.

A Painful Experience

Surviving Suicide Loss of a loved one to suicide is perhaps the most painful of human experiences. The pain of the loss of someone to suicide is never totally ameliorated. It is always there, and the survivor's eye is quick to find it. It only becomes tolerable as the thread of loss is woven into the fabric of the survivor's life with threads of more happy moments. Few understand that the death is seldom self-determined, but rather driven by a distortion of perception by a biochemical defect.

Surviving is wrought by confused feelings. Guilt, grief, anger, and despair increase survivors' own risk of self-inflicted death. Each day they may play the game of if's: "What if I said or did that?" "What if I didn't?" Survivor groups help those left behind to learn what feelings to expect, and to learn the course of grief.

Most suicides are preventable if the psychiatric disorders responsible for clinical symptoms and impulsivity are identified early and treated aggressively, and psychosocial stress factors are reduced through therapy. However, a clinician is not omnipotent. Profoundly despairing people can lie about plans and hoard medicine even if prescribed cautiously. The best care for potentially suicidal patients is initial and recurrent assessment of risk, timely intervention, and the provision of support to those especially at risk, regardless of the presence of symptoms.

Bibliography

Books

David Aldridge	*Suicide: The Tragedy of Hopelessness*. London: Jessica Kingsley, 1998.
Margaret Pabst Battin	*Ethical Issues in Suicide*. Englewood Cliffs, NJ: Prentice-Hall, 1995.
Victor Cosculluela	*The Ethics of Suicide*. New York: Garland, 1995.
Robert Firestone	*Suicide and the Inner Voice*. Thousand Oaks, CA: Sage, 1997.
Herbert Hendin	*Seduced by Death: Doctors, Patients, and the Dutch Cure*. New York: W.W. Norton, 1998.
Derek Humphry and Mary Clement	*Freedom to Die: People, Politics, and the Right-to-Die Movement*. New York: St. Martin's, 1998.
David Lester	*Making Sense of Suicide: An In-Depth Look at Why People Kill Themselves*. Philadelphia: Charles Press, 1997.
Robert Emmet Long, ed.	*Suicide*. New York: H.W. Wilson, 1995.
John T. Maltsberger and Mark J. Goldblatt, eds.	*Essential Papers on Suicide*. New York: New York University Press, 1996.
Sheila McLean and Alison Britton	*The Case for Physician Assisted Suicide*. London: HarperCollins, 1997.
Paul R. Robbins	*Adolescent Suicide*. Jefferson, NC: McFarland & Company, 1998.
Edwin S. Shneidman	*The Suicidal Mind*. New York: Oxford University Press, 1996.
Morton M. Silverman and Ronald W. Maris, eds.	*Suicide Prevention Toward the Year 2000*. New York: Guilford, 1995.
James L. Werth Jr., ed.	*Contemporary Perspectives on Rational Suicide*. Philadelphia: Taylor and Francis, 1999.
Mark G. Williams	*Cry of Pain: Understanding Suicide and Self-Harm*. New York: Penguin Books, 1997.

Bibliography

Periodicals

Marcia Angell and Kathleen Foley	"The Supreme Court and Physician-Assisted Suicide—The Ultimate Right," *New England Journal of Medicine*, January 2, 1997. Available from 10 Shattuck St., Boston, MA 02115-6094.
Johann Christoph Arnold	"Talking About Suicide," *Plough*, Autumn 1998. Available from Spring Valley Bruderhof, Farmington, PA 15437-9506.
J. Bottum	"Debriefing the Philosophers," *First Things*, June/July 1997. Available from 156 Fifth Ave., Suite 400, New York, NY 10010.
Erwin Chemerinsky	"A Right to Physician-Assisted Suicide?" *Trial*, September 1997.
Richard E. Coleson	"The Glucksberg & Quill Amicus Curiae Briefs, Verbatim Arguments Opposing Assisted Suicide," *Issues in Law & Medicine*, August 1, 1997.
Nicholas Dixon	"On the Difference Between Physician-Assisted Suicide and Active Euthanasia," *Hastings Center Report*, September/October 1998.
Barbara Dority	"Physician Aid in Dying: Within Some of Our Lifetimes?" *Humanist*, September/October 1997.
Steve Hallock	"Physician-Assisted Suicide: 'Slippery Slope' or Civil Right?" *Humanist*, July 17, 1996.
Herbert Hendin, Kathleen Foley, and Margot White	"Physician-Assisted Suicide: Reflections on Oregon's First Case," *Issues in Law & Medicine*, vol. 14, no. 3, Winter 1998.
Russell Hittinger	"Assisted Suicide: No and Yes, but Mainly Yes," *First Things*, March 1997.
Yale Kamisar	"The Reasons So Many People Support Physician-Assisted Suicide—and Why These Reasons Are Not Convincing," *Issues in Law & Medicine*, September 1, 1996.
Leon R. Kass	"Dehumanization Triumphant," *First Things*, August/September 1996.
Leon R. Kass and Nelson Lund	"Courting Death: Assisted Suicide, Doctors and the Law," *Commentary*, December 1996.
Jerome P. Kassirer	"The Supreme Court and Physician-Assisted Suicide—The Ultimate Right," *New England Journal of Medicine*, January 2, 1997.
Mark G. Kuczewski	"Physician-Assisted Death: Can Philosophical Bioethics Aid Social Policy?" *Cambridge Quarterly of Healthcare Ethics*, Fall 1998. Available from Cambridge University Press, 40 W. 20th St., New York, NY 10011-4211.
Alexandra Dylan Lowe	"Facing the Final Exit," *ABA Journal*, September 1997.
Thomas Maier	"An Ethicist Explains the Dutch Way of Death," *Newsday*, April 4, 1997.

Suicide

Alexandra Marks — "Rise in Teen Suicides Spurs New Solutions," *Christian Science Monitor*, March 5, 1997.

Diane E. Meier et al. — "A National Survey of Physician-Assisted Suicide and Euthanasia in the United States," *New England Journal of Medicine*, vol. 338, no. 17, April 23, 1998.

Jennifer Mendelsohn and William Knaus — "Last Passage," *People Weekly*, February 19, 1996.

National Legal Center for the Dependent and Medically Disabled — "Assisted Suicide: A Disability Perspective," *Issues in Law & Medicine*, January 5, 1999.

National Legal Center for the Dependent and Medically Disabled — "Physician-Assisted Suicide and Euthanasia in the Netherlands: A Report to the House Judiciary Subcommittee on the Constitution Executive Summary," *Issues in Law & Medicine*, January 5, 1999.

David Novak — "Suicide Is Not a Private Choice," *First Things*, August/September 1997.

Kevin P. Quinn — "Assisted Suicide and Equal Protection: In Defense of the Distinction Between Killing and Letting Die," *Issues in Law & Medicine*, November 1, 1997.

John P. Safranek — "Autonomy and Assisted Suicide: The Execution of Freedom," *Hastings Center Report*, July/August 1998.

Joseph E. Shapiro — "Euthanasia's Home," *U.S. News & World Report*, July/August 1998.

Don Sloan — "The Politics of Doctor-Assisted Suicide," *Political Affairs*, May 1997.

Michael Stingl — "Euthanasia and Health Reform in Canada," *Cambridge Quarterly of Healthcare Ethics*, Fall 1998.

Dorothy B. Trippel — "Good Death Can Be a Sacred Gift," *Friends Journal*, October 1997. Available from 1216 Arch St., 2A, Philadelphia, PA 19107-2835.

Michael B. Uhlmann — "The Legal Logic of Euthanasia," *First Things*, June/July 1996.

Ernest van den Haag — "Why Does Suicide Have a Bad Reputation?" *Chronicles*, August 1998. Available from 928 N. Main St., Rockford, IL 61103.

Adam Wolfson — "Killing Off the Dying?" *Public Interest*, April 15, 1998.

Organizations to Contact

The editors have compiled the following list of organizations concerned with the issues debated in this book. The descriptions are derived from materials provided by the organizations. All have publications or information available for interested readers. The list was compiled on the date of publication of the present volume; the information provided here may change. Be aware that many organizations take several weeks or longer to respond to inquiries, so allow as much time as possible.

American Association of Suicidology (AAS)
4201 Connecticut Ave. NW, Ste. 408, Washington, DC 20008
(202) 237-2280 • fax: (202) 237-2282
e-mail: debbiehu@ix.netcom.com • website: http://www.suicidology.org

The association is one of the largest suicide prevention organizations in the United States. It promotes the view that suicidal thoughts are almost always a symptom of depression and that suicide is almost never a rational decision. In addition to prevention of suicide, the group also works to increase public awareness about suicide and to help those grieving the death of a loved one to suicide. The association publishes the quarterly newsletters *American Association of Suicidology—Newslink* and *Surviving Suicide*, and the quarterly journal *Suicide and Life Threatening Behavior.*

American Foundation for Suicide Prevention (AFSP)
120 Wall Street, 22nd Fl., New York, NY 10005
(888) 333-2377 • fax: (212) 363-6237
e-mail: rfabrika@afsp.org • website: http://www.afsp.org

Formerly known as the American Suicide Foundation, the AFSP supports scientific research on depression and suicide, educates the public and professionals on the recognition and treatment of depressed and suicidal individuals, and provides support programs for those coping with the loss of a loved one to suicide. It opposes the legalization of physician-assisted suicide. AFSP publishes a policy statement on physician-assisted suicide, the newsletter *Crisis,* and the quarterly *Lifesavers.*

American Life League (ALL)
PO Box 1350, Stafford, VA 22555
(540) 659-4171 • fax: (540) 659-2586
e-mail: whylife@all.org • website: http://www.all.org

The league believes that human life is sacred. It works to educate Americans about the dangers of all forms of euthanasia and opposes legislative efforts that would legalize or increase its incidence. It publishes the bimonthly pro-life magazine *Celebrate Life,* and distributes videos, brochures, and newsletters monitoring euthanasia-related developments.

American Psychiatric Association
1400 K St. NW, Washington, DC 20005
(202) 682-6000 • fax: (202) 682-6850
e-mail: apa@psych.org • website: http://www.psych.org

An organization of psychiatrists dedicated to studying the nature, treatment, and prevention of mental disorders, the APA helps create mental health policies, distributes information about psychiatry, and promotes psychiatric research and education. It publishes the *American Journal of Psychiatry* and *Psychiatric News* monthly.

American Psychological Association (APA)

750 First St. NE, Washington, DC 20002-4242
(202) 336-5500 • fax: (202) 336-5708
e-mail: public.affairs@apa.org • web address: http://www.apa.org

This professional organization for psychologists aims to "advance psychology as a science, as a profession, and as a means of promoting human welfare." It produces numerous publications, including the book *Adolescent Suicide: Assessment and Intervention*, the report "Researcher Links Perfectionism in High Achievers with Depression and Suicide," and the online guide *Warning Signs—A Violence Prevention Guide for Youth*.

Canadian Association for Suicide Prevention (CASP)

#301, 11456 Jasper Ave. NW, Edmonton, AB, T5K 0M1 Canada
(780) 482-0198 • fax: (780) 488-1495
e-mail: casp@suicideprevention.ca
website: http://www.compusmart.ab.ca/supnet/casp.htm

CASP organizes annual conferences and educational programs on suicide prevention. It publishes the newsletter *CASP News* three times a year and the booklet *Suicide Prevention in Canadian Schools*.

Choice in Dying (CID)

1035 30th Street NW, Washington, DC 20007
(800) 989-9455 • (202) 338-0242 • fax: (202) 338-9790
e-mail: cid@choices.org • website: http://www.choices.org

Choice in Dying is a national, not-for-profit organization dedicated to fostering communication about complex end-of-life decisions among individuals, their loved ones, and health care professionals. The organization invented living wills in 1967 and provides the only national hotline to respond to families and patients during end-of-life crises. CID also provides educational materials, public and professional education, and ongoing monitoring of changes in state and federal right-to-die legislation.

Compassion in Dying Federation

PMB 415, 6312 SW Capitol Hwy., Portland, OR 97201
(503) 221-9556 • fax: (503) 228-9610
e-mail: info@compassionindying.org • website: http://www.compassionindying.org

The mission of Compassion in Dying Federation is to provide national leadership for client service, legal advocacy, and public education to improve pain and symptom management, increase patient empowerment and self-determination, and expand end-of-life choices to include aid-in-dying for terminally ill, mentally competent adults. It publishes periodic newsletters, press releases, and testimonials.

Depression and Related Affective Disorders Association (DRADA)

Meyer 3-181, 600 N. Wolfe St., Baltimore, MD 21287-7381
(410) 955-4647
e-mail: drada@jhmi.edu • website: http://www.med.jhu.edu/drada

DRADA, a nonprofit organization that works in cooperation with the Department of Psychiatry at the Johns Hopkins University School of Medicine, seeks to alleviate the suffering arising from depression and manic depression by assisting self-help groups, providing education and information, and lending support to research programs. It publishes the report "A Look at . . . Suicide, a Relentless and Underrated Foe" and the book *Night Falls Fast—Understanding Suicide*.

Euthanasia Prevention Coalition BC
103-2609 Westview Dr., Ste. 126, North Vancouver, BC V7N 4N2 Canada
(604) 795-3772 • fax: (604) 794-3960
e-mail: info@epc.bc.ca • website: http://www.epc.bc.ca

The Euthanasia Prevention Coalition opposes the promotion or legalization of euthanasia and assisted suicide. The coalition's purpose is to educate the public on risks associated with the promotion of euthanasia, increase public awareness of alternative methods for the relief of suffering, and to represent the vulnerable as an advocate before the courts on issues of euthanasia and related subjects. Press releases from the coalition are available at its website.

Foundation of Thanatology
630 W. 168th St., New York, NY 10032
(212) 928-2066 • fax: (718) 549-7219

This organization of health, theology, psychology, and social science professionals is devoted to scientific and humanist inquiries into health, loss, grief, and bereavement. The foundation coordinates professional, educational, and research programs concerned with mortality and grief. It publishes the periodicals *Advances in Thanatology* and *Archives of the Foundation of Thanatology*.

The Hemlock Society
PO Box 101810, Denver, CO 80250
(800) 247-7421 • (303) 639-1202 • fax: (303) 639-1224
e-mail: hemlock@privatei.com • website: http://www.hemlock.org

The society believes that terminally ill individuals have the right to commit suicide. The society publishes books on suicide, death, and dying, including *Final Exit*, a guide for those suffering with terminal illnesses and considering suicide. The Hemlock Society also publishes the newsletter *TimeLines*.

International Anti-Euthanasia Task Force (IAETF)
PO Box 760, Steubenville, OH 43952
(740) 282-3810
e-mail: info@iaetf.org • website: http://www.iaetf.org

The task force opposes euthanasia, assisted suicide, and policies that threaten the lives of the medically vulnerable. IAETF publishes fact sheets and position papers on euthanasia-related topics in addition to the bimonthly newsletter *IAETF Update*. It analyzes the policies and legislation concerning medical and social work organizations and files *amicus curiae* briefs in major "right-to-die" cases.

National Alliance for the Mentally Ill (NAMI)
200 N. Glebe Rd., Ste. 1015, Arlington, VA 22203-3754
(800) 950-6264 • fax: (703) 524-9094
website: http://www.nami.org

NAMI is a consumer advocacy and support organization composed largely of family members of people with severe mental illnesses such as schizophrenia, manic-depressive illness, and depression. The alliance adheres to the position that severe mental illnesses are biological brain diseases and that mentally ill people should not be blamed or stigmatized for their conditions. NAMI favors increased government funding for research, treatment, and community services for the mentally ill. Its publications include the bimonthly newsletter *NAMI Advocate*, as well as various brochures, handbooks, and policy recommendations.

National Depressive and Manic-Depressive Association (NDMDA)

730 N. Franklin St., Ste. 501, Chicago, IL 60610-3526
(800) 826-3632 • (312) 642-0049 • fax: (312) 642-7243
e-mail: arobinson@ndmda.org • website: http://www.ndmda.org

The association provides support and advocacy for patients with depression and manic-depressive illness. It seeks to persuade the public that these disorders are biochemical in nature and to end the stigmatization of people who suffer from them. It publishes the quarterly *NDMDA Newsletter* and various books and pamphlets.

National Foundation for Depressive Illness (NAFDI)

PO Box 2257, New York, NY 10116
(800) 239-1265
website: http://www.depression.org

NAFDI informs the public, health care providers, and corporations about depression and manic-depressive illness. It promotes the view that these disorders are physical illnesses treatable with medication, and it believes that such medication should be made readily available to those who need it. The foundation maintains several toll-free telephone lines and distributes brochures, bibliographies, and literature on the symptoms of and treatments for depression and manic-depressive illness. It also publishes the quarterly newsletter *NAFDI News*.

National Hospice Organization (NHO)

1700 Diagonal Rd., Ste. 300, Alexandria, VA 22314
(800) 658-8898 • (703) 243-5900 • fax: (703) 525-5762
e-mail: drsnho@cais.org • website: http://www.nho.org

The organization works to educate the public about the benefits of hospice care for the terminally ill and their families. It seeks to promote the idea that with the proper care and pain medication, the terminally ill can live out their lives comfortably and in the company of their families. The organization opposes euthanasia and assisted suicide. It conducts educational and training programs for administrators and caregivers in numerous aspects of hospice care. It publishes the quarterlies *Hospice Journal* and *Hospice Magazine*, as well as books and monographs.

Samaritans

10 The Grove, Slough, Berkshire SL1 1QP UK
01753 216500 • fax: 01753 775787
e-mail: jo@samaritans.org • website: http://www.samaritans.org.uk

Samaritans is the largest suicide prevention organization in the world. Established in England in 1953, the organization now has branches in at least forty-four nations throughout the world. The group's volunteers provide counseling and other assistance to suicidal and despondent individuals. In addition, Samaritans publishes the booklets *Elderly Suicide, Teen Suicide Information and Guidelines for Parents*, and *The Suicidal Student: A Guide for Educators*.

SA\VE—Suicide Awareness\Voices of Education

PO Box 24507, Minneapolis, MN 55424-0507
(612) 946-7998
e-mail: save@winternet.com • website: http://www.save.org

SA\VE works to prevent suicide and to help those grieving after the suicide of a loved one. Its members believe that brain diseases, such as depression, should be detected and treated promptly because they can result in suicide. In addition to pamphlets and the book *Suicide: Survivors—A Guide for Those Left Behind*, the organization publishes the quarterly newsletter *Voices*.

Suicide Information and Education Centre (SIEC)
#201, 1615 10th Ave. SW, Calgary, AB T3C 0J7 Canada
(403) 245-3900 • fax: (403) 245-0299
e-mail: siec@siec.ca • website: http://www.siec.ca

The Suicide Information and Education Centre acquires and distributes information on suicide prevention. It maintains a computerized database, a free mailing list, and a document delivery service. It publishes the quarterly *Current Awareness Bulletin* and the monthly *SIEC Clipping Service*.

Index

DATE DUE

11-30			

Demco, Inc. 38-294